MOU BIKE GUIDE

to

Mid Yorkshire
Rye Dale & the Wolds

by
DENNIS E LIVERSIDGE

THE ERNEST PRESS

Published by The Ernest Press 1998
© Dennis E Liversidge

ISBN 0 948153 51 2

British Library Cataloguing-in-Publication Data has been registered
with the British Library in Wetherby and is available on request.

Typeset by Stanningley Serif
Printed by St Edmundsbury Press

CONTENTS.

Route distances

Aberford - Towton - Barkston Ash.	14.5	Miles
Tadcaster - Nova Scotia Loop.	15	Miles
Scagglethorpe Moor - Ouse Bridleway.	13.5	Miles
Crockey Hill - Esckrick.	14	Miles
York Cycleway - Rickall - Skipwith Common.	19.5	Miles
Welburn - Castle Howard.	17	Miles
Slingsby - Caulkleys Bank - Barton Moor.	15	Miles
Hovingham Park - Grimston Moor.	11.75	Miles
Marton-In-The-Forest.	14	Miles
The Becks Circle.	14	Miles
Givendale - Warter Wold - Huggate Heads.	24	Miles
Fridaythorpe - North Dalton.	23	Miles
Grimston Brow - Wolds Way - Thixendale.	16.5	Miles
Dunnington - Elvington.	13.5	Miles
Rievaulx - Whitestone Cliff	19.5	Miles
Beadlam - Pockley Moor - Ruddland Rigg.	21	Miles
Sinnington - Rosedale Abbey.	19.5	Miles
Sinnington - Cropton Forest.	24	Miles
White Horse Loop	15	Miles
Stony Moor - Newton Dale - Blansby Park.	16.5	Miles

Route gradings

Aberford - Towton - Barkston Ash.	2/2
Tadcaster - Nova Scotia Loop.	1/1
Scagglethorpe Moor - Ouse Bridleway.	2/2
Crockey Hill - Esckrick.	1/2
York Cycleway - Rickall - Skipwith Common.	1/2
Welburn - Castle Howard.	3/3
Slingsby - Caulkleys Bank - Barton Moor.	2/3
Hovingham Park - Grimston Moor.	2/2
Marton-In-The-Forest.	1/2
The Becks Circle.	2/3
Givendale - Warter Wold - Huggate Heads.	3/3
Fridaythorpe - North Dalton.	3/3
Grimston Brow - Wolds Way - Thixendale.	3/3
Dunnington - Elvington.	2/2
Rievaulx - Whitestone Cliff	3/4
Beadlam - Pockley Moor - Ruddland Rigg.	3/3
Sinnington - Rosedale Abbey.	3/3
Sinnington - Cropton Forest.	3/3
White Horse Loop	3/4
Stony Moor - Newton Dale - Blansby Park.	3/3

ACKNOWLEDGEMENTS.

Compiling a number of Mountain Bike routes for any specific area is not always easy without the help and assistance of family and friends. So, I would like to express sincere thanks to the following -

The officers of the city of York County Council Highways and the Rights of Way Dept at Fulford Lodge.
The officers of Pickering Highways and Public Rights of Way Dept.
The Highways Dept at Kirby Moorside.
The officers of North York Moors National Park Authority (rights of way) in Helmsley.
The Forestry Commission, Pickering for access permission over their lands on certain routes.

Mike Ellis, Phil Ewart, Martin Jagger, John Berry, Sid Quirk, Maurice Legood, Chris Grayshon-Pedley and members of the West Yorkshire Rough Riders who assisted with route checking, transport and encouragement.

Cover photographs courtesy of John Lister L.B.I.P.P.

I am also indebted to John Lister for his help with proof-reading and correction

INTRODUCTION.

Yorkshire, being one of the largest counties in England, boasts hundreds of miles of legal off-road routes. Many of these bridleways and bye-ways have been explored and recorded for mountain bikers to follow. Mid Yorkshire, Ryedale and the Yorkshire Wolds are areas which have not quite received the same attention from mountain bikers as have adjacent areas. With this in mind, I have researched these areas carefully to fill the gap in the collection of Yorkshire Mountain Bike guide books now available.

In order to define the area more specifically, I have chosen to refer to the A1 Trunk road, running north-south, as a boundary line, and look at the region to the east of this line, extending as far north as Helmsley and Pickering, including Ryedale, and as far south as the York Wolds. This is the area I have covered for the off-road routes in the book. Some of the more northerly routes venture into the lower region of the North York Moors and the Hambleton Hills, but only just. Those routes further south, explore tracks and bridleways in the Yorkshire Wolds and even some routes in the Vale of York. The area is at present, like many others, beginning to receive attention from Mountain Bikers, many of whom will be seeking new, and relatively untouched bridleways and tracks, in an attempt to move away from the tried and tested routes of neighbouring counties.

The York Wolds are not as severe in nature as Derbyshire's Peak District or the Yorkshire Dales. The unique topography of rolling hills and valleys, softened by the woodlands and meadows, that seems unchanged with time, serves to conceal farms and villages within its folds. As you move north from the York Wolds and head towards Pickering, you cross the vale of York, a flat expanse of open countryside. (Thousands of years ago, this area was

covered by a huge glacial lake.) The trails in this area are somewhat flat, but still enjoyable and ideal for the novice rider or even a
family group just visiting the area.

The A170 trunk road, running from Helmsley in the west to
Pickering in the east, is where you will meet the lower end of the
North York Moors and Ryedale. The more experienced or fitter rider,
will find the routes here more challenging, though the novice rider
will, hopefully, progress to this area. The topography is typical of
regions affected by the action of past Ice Ages. The valleys are 'U'
shaped, the Moors are rounded off, gouged and smoothed by a
massive ice field, which covered the area thousands of years ago
leaving behind a Mountain Biker's paradise of climbs and long descents.

TRAIL CODE OF CONDUCT.
We must remember at all times, that bridleways and public tracks
are there for all to use, so please be polite to others using the same
trail, particularly walkers and horse riders. If the track is narrow,
slow down or stop and allow them to continue first. A walker leap-
ing to one side, or a horse rider having to calm a frightened mount,
due to thoughtless riding by a Mountain Biker, will do nothing to
help the image of Mountain Biking, or the safety of all concerned.

Conservation of the countryside should be foremost in the minds
of everyone. Many tracks are being rapidly eroded because of mis-
use. Try to stick to the trail. Avoid taking short cuts, such as a detour around wet sections, via grass or heather sections off to the
side. Half the fun can be found by trying to 'clean' the muddy sections. So go for it !

If you find yourself in a situation where your right of way on a
route is being questioned, please be diplomatic. Explain why you
are there, use your O.S. map to support your reasons, but do not

incite a riot. Retire politely and check later with the appropriate authority. Let them take action if it is necessary.

There are many guide lines, as well as common sense, which suggest how we should conduct ourselves when riding off road. The following are those in common usage:

The Country Code. (Issued by the Countryside Commission and intended for walkers, horse riders and other users of the countryside, but which should also be followed by all cyclists where appropriate).
The code states :
Enjoy the countryside and respect its life and work.
Guard against risk of fire.
Fasten all gates.
Keep your dogs under control.
Keep to public paths across farm land.
Use gates and stiles to cross fences, hedges and walls.
Leave livestock, crops and machinery alone.
Lake your litter home.
Help keep all water clean.
Protect wildlife, plants and trees.
Take special care on country roads.
Make no unnecessary noise.

There is a code more specifically for Mountain Biking Off-Road (issued by the British Mountain Bike Federation).
The code states :
Only ride where you know you have a legal right.
Always yield to horses and pedestrians.
Avoid animals and crops. In some circumstances this may not be possible, at which times contact should be kept to a minimum.

Take all litter with you.
Leave all gates as found.
Keep the noise down.
Don't get annoyed with anyone; it never solves any problems.
Always try to be self-sufficient, for you and your bike.
Never create a fire hazard.

ROUTE INFORMATION.
Because of the diverse nature of the routes in the book, each will begin with a brief overview. This should help cyclists to decide whether or not they wish to attempt the ride, without reading through all the route notes. A simple grading system can be used to reflect the difficulty of the route, the easiest being graded 1, the hardest 5. Because routes vary in distance and terrain, a long route may be classed as grade 2 simply because it is relatively flat and the terrain makes it easy riding. On the other hand, a short route may be graded 4, as the riding is technically more demanding because of the terrain. From these two extremes, it can be seen that a twofold system of grading must be used — hence you will find a grade for physical difficulty, and a grade for technical difficulty (in that order). This method will be used at the beginning of each ride, e.g. 2/2, which would suggest a relatively easy route with few technical problems for an average rider, with perhaps a couple of years experience. However, this is only a rough guide and some may find that it does not meet their interpretation of a hard or easy route.

Route legality was my priority and all the routes have been ridden and re-checked, since one ride became a nonstarter shortly after I had ridden it legally. This was because a section was downgraded from a bridleway to a footpath. Routes should be checked before riding if there is any doubt. New sections will appear and old sections will be downgraded, or vanish completely from time to time. Please remember that cyclists are not allowed to ride on Footpaths.

I would suggest that the following maps should be used in conjunction with the sketch maps printed in this book: Ordinance Survey maps - 1:25 000 Pathfinder series, or 1:50 000 Landranger series.

Much more time and money is being invested in new off-road cycle-ways, thanks to the £42.5 million Lottery-funded grant from the Millennium Commission. The civil engineering charity, Sustrans, is building the National Cycle Network. Local Authority planners such as the City of York Council, have already made much progress in improving the lot of cyclists by providing cycle tracks within the city, and by converting disused rail tracks into cycle and walkways. Other councils are beginning to follow York's example, and are starting to open up much of the countryside to cyclists, by developing existing bridleways and upgrading many other tracks and pathways.

TIMES.
These, again, are a rough guide and do not include stops. They are, perhaps, the times a rider of average fitness would take for each route.

ABBREVIATIONS:

L	Left	BW	Bridleway
R	Right	FP	Footpath
J	Junction	N,S,E,W	North etc.
TJ	T-junction		
XR	Crossroads		
SO	Straight on		
ST	Single track		

MAP SYMBOLS

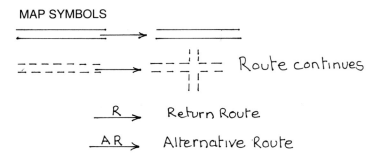

R → Return Route

AR → Alternative Route

EQUIPMENT.

Like all specialised sports, selecting the correct equipment is important if you wish to get off to a good start. Mountain Biking is no exception.

THE BIKE.

This is the one single piece of equipment which is indispensable; your choice of machine will influence the outcome of your rides. A bike capable of coping with a variety of conditions and terrain would be ideal, even essential, on some of the routes. A heavy and unwieldy bike can be soul destroying and may even put you off riding a bike for good. Obviously you should buy a mountain bike within your budget, but seek advice from a specialist Mountain Bike shop, or experienced Mountain Biker, before you buy.

Do not assume that you will require the same sized frame as you would use on a road bike. The Mountain Bike frame is much smaller and gives provision for stand-over clearance at the top tube. The commonest mistake is to buy a bike which is too big , this can lead to all sorts of problems when you start riding off road. As a rough guide 2 to 3 inches of clearance is needed between your crotch and the top tube, when stood astride the bike.

If regular checks are made and the bike is looked after, there is less chance of it letting you down, once you are out on the trail. Neglected areas are usually the chain and gear train. These tend to be the most vulnerable parts and the most difficult to clean. Check them carefully, clean and lubricate them regularly. The same applies to the cables, these should be replaced if any signs of wear are beginning to show. You don't want to find yourself out in the country without gears or brakes! Regular care of your bike will pay dividends; it will respond well when you want it to. Try to use a routine check list so that all nuts, bolts and fastenings are tightened if necessary. Check the tyre wear — they may look fine one week and the next time you look, they appear almost bald !

Don't be caught out on the trail because you forgot to check your equipment before you left. Your friends won't thank you either, particularly if they are waiting for you in the rain !

TOOLS.
If you should have the misfortune to break down when you are out on the trail, a tool kit will come in handy, providing it's not a major mishap. Without question, you should carry a number of useful tools and spares on any ride, even the shortest near home.

Always carry a spare inner tube and a couple of tyre levers. A puncture repair outfit would be useful backup as well, but don't forget your pump, with appropriate valve connection! Most Mountain Bike manufactures use equipment with Metric size threads on their fastenings. A selection of good quality Metric spanners; 6,8,9 and 10 mm, would be most useful, particularly for brakes and gears. Similarly, a suitable selection of Allen keys would also be useful for seat pillar, bars and stem etc. A small screwdriver, a spoke key, a chain splitter and some spare links, and a small selection of useful nuts and bolts should be added.

Be careful with your selection of tools. Remember you have to carry them, and even more important, know how to use them. For much longer rides or tours, a more comprehensive kit could be put together to suite your own requirements.

Carrying the tools need not be a problem. A small, weatherproof, light but strong container, which can be easily tucked away under the back of the saddle, is ideal. Improvise if you have to. For my own use, a small, cylindrical, redundant pencil case, made from a nylon waterproof material, has survived many years as a tool-kit carrier.

CLOTHING.

The choice of garments for Mountain Bike riding can vary from the close-fitting Lycra material favoured by road cyclists to the more laid-back loose-fit, baggy shorts and shirts often worn by the new generation of Mountain Bikers. It is essential to remember that whatever style you choose you have adequate protection from inclement weather. Ideally you should carry with you either a waterproof, or at least showerproof, garment.

In the more hilly regions the weather can change quite quickly. Without proper protection from the elements, you could find yourself in difficulties. Fortunately, on nearly all of the routes in this guide book, you are never far from civilisation, should you encounter any problems.

Ideally cycling shorts with a padded insert are best for comfortable riding.

Many off-road riders prefer to wear purpose-made Mountain Bike shoes or boots as opposed to trainers or other footwear, which tend to make your legs and feet ache prematurely. Recent developments in fast-wicking (the garment's ability to quickly remove sweat from the skin's surface to the outside layer) underclothing, means you no longer have quite the same problem with the chill factor, when you start to cool down after a long uphill climb. This type of garment is well worth investing in, especially if you ride in the winter months.

It would be possible to write much more about what Mountain Bike specific clothing to wear but this is not within the scope of this book. If you wish to find out more, seek advice from experts in the Mountain Biking field.

FIRST-AID AND PERSONAL SAFETY.

I do not feel qualified to offer professional advice regarding first-aid, but I would suggest that it is essential to have some knowledge of first-aid. If you are a regular rider and ride with friends, encourage someone in the group to attend a course run by a recognised organisation such St Johns Ambulance etc. However if this is not possible, it would still be helpful for one rider to carry a small first-aid kit comprising plasters, mediwipes, a selection of bandages, micropore tape and safety pins.

Mountain Biking is best undertaken in groups of two or more, so that in the event of one person being injured and unable to continue riding, other rider(s) could be employed to seek help, leaving the immobilised rider in as warm and comfortable a state as is possible. The advantage of having more than two riders is that one rider can stay with the injured party whilst the others seek help. It is also important that riders carry an address and telephone number of a person to contact in the event of injury as well as any other relevant medical information which could be useful to a doctor or paramedic. It would be useful to read any literature which deals with safety in the mountains or countryside.

15

16

17

HELMSLEY

RYE DALE

19

8

9

YORK.

2

3

4

5

1

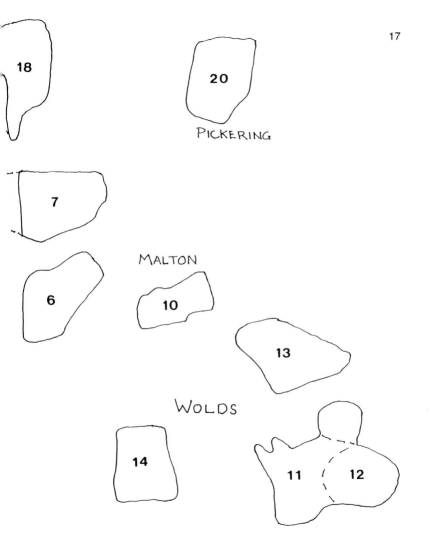

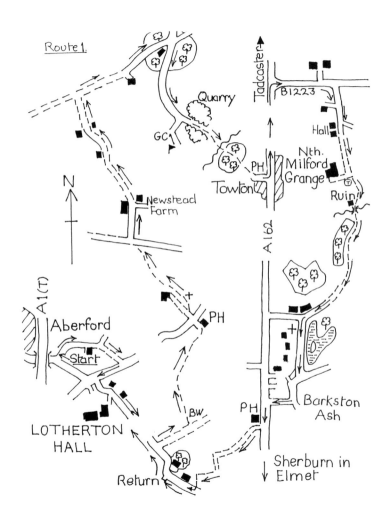

Route 1.

Tadcaster
B1223
Quarry
Hall
GC
Nth.
Milford
Grange
PH
Ruin
Towton
N
A162
Newstead
Farm
A1(T)
+
PH
Aberford
Start
BW
PH
Barkston
Ash
LOTHERTON
HALL
Sherburn in
Elmet
Return

Route 1   ABERFORD-TOWTON-BARKSTON ASH.

Distance	14.5 miles; off road 9.5 miles; on road 5 miles.
Time	2 hours, to 2 hours 30 mins.
Grade	2/2
Terrain	Farm land, woodland, undulating but not unduly difficult - open fields in places.
Surface	Tarmac Lanes, farm tracks with rough surface, Single track through woods, Grassy undefined tracks.
Maps	O.S. map Sheet 105 Landranger Series.

This is not a particularly difficult route, but it offers many surprises as you follow it. The landscape is not quite as flat as you would expect for this area, in fact at one point there is a testing single track climb through a wooded section, which the experienced rider will find entertaining and the novice will find difficult.

The start of the ride is not far from the A1 trunk road in Aberford, so access from distant counties is quite easy. The village of Aberford is quite picturesque and features on part of another trail to the west (see Rte 13; MBG West Yorks). Link the two together and you have quite a long off-road route.

THE ROUTE.
From the start GR 430369, go under the A1 on the road signposted Lotherton Hall. Shortly after the A1 bridge, on the bend as you start to climb, turn L following this road. As the surface changes from smooth to rough, it passes a small house on the right. Bear R at a junction, ignoring the left track up to a farm. Go up the track until it emerges at a TJ with a road. Turn R, follow the road to a signpost pointing to Sherburn-in-Elmet.

Turn L and continue for just over a mile before turning L again. Go up this open road and after 50 yards, you will see a BW sign on the L. This is an undefined track leading diagonally across an open field towards a hedge and running parallel to overhead power lines on the right. Follow it as it levels off and begins to drop steadily towards a main road at a TJ. On the corner of this junction is the Crooked Billet Public House. Cross the road, taking care to watch out for fast-moving traffic, and go into an entrance where, on the right, is a BW. This is Chantry Lane, so called because of the mysterious little church that resides in the middle of the field, which you are about to enter via a metal gate. Go L through the field alongside the hedge. The track is not very distinct, but at the end of the hedge, overlooking Lead Hall Farm, is a small wooden gateway. Go L through the gate and immediately R, following the track to a TJ. Go L then after 50 yards go R, at the signpost to Hayton Farm. Continue down this track to Newstead Farm. Do not turn off but follow the track SO until it reaches a TJ at the top of a moderate climb. Go R down this long descent. On reaching a house set back on the right, keep to the L and continue up the track which eventually levels off, before dropping gently down to the old school house at an offset XR.

Stutton, a small hamlet, is only 1/2 mile SO at the XR, if you require a rest or a refuel. If not, go sharp R, almost back on yourself, and continue along the tarmac lane for 1/2 mile until you arrive at a sign for the local golf club. Go down the track to the left of the sign, where you will see quarry workings on either side of the trail, and a metal barrier. This is a narrow ST running down through woods to a 'hop on, hop off' wooden bridge, crossing Cock Beck. Soon the track winds its way up a slope, which could become quite slippery after wet weather. At the top it opens out into a field and then improves as it heads towards a pub at a TJ. This is the main road through Towton Village. Go L along the main road for 1/2 mile, turning R at the signpost to Selby and Ulleskelf. Continue along this road for just over a mile. Look out for a farm on your left, and soon after, at a minor XR, go R to North Milford (signpost).

Continue along this easy lane, passing North Milford Hall on your right, then shortly afterwards, as the lane turns to the right and on to a large farm (North Milford Grange), you will see a telegraph pole (see [T] on map at GR506386) directly in front of you bearing the sign 'Sherburn Model Club'. Go L then R. The BW has been redirected, so that it now crosses the field ahead of you.

This part of the route is a bit complicated because the temporary track is not always obvious. However, by working your way around the field you will come to an irrigation ditch. Follow this ditch to a small bridge by a ruined building at GR505382. (In its normal state, the bridleway goes SO from the telegraph pole and crosses the field towards the ruined building.) Cross the bridge onto a rough track bearing R. The track is rough at this point, but as it nears a golf course, which can be seen through trees to the right, it begins to improve. When the track eventually emerges at Scarthingwell, near a collection of cottages and farms, take the road through an open gateway. Do not be put off by the sign at the entrance, this road is for public use. (If you wish, though, you can continue to the main road and turn L to Barkston Ash.) Otherwise continue along the aforementioned road through the open gateway, passing the Catholic Church on the right and continuing through to Barkston Ash Village. Bear R through the village, past the Boot and Shoe public house with its reputed ghost, and continue up to a TJ. This a main road, so again take care as you turn L. Follow it for a short distance to another pub, the Ash Tree, on the right. Just after the pub, turn R down Oldgates Lane and continue along this BW until it emerges, after a downhill run, at a TJ.

Go R and follow this road as it heads back towards Lotherton Hall. You should now recognise where you are (hopefully), having covered this part of the route earlier. At the staggered XR, go L for the quick road back to Aberford and the starting point, or turn R and follow the road for 200 yds before turning L down a track which you came up earlier. This track will take you back to the start at Aberford.

Bridleway near Barkston Ash.

Bilton Village

Healaugh Priory

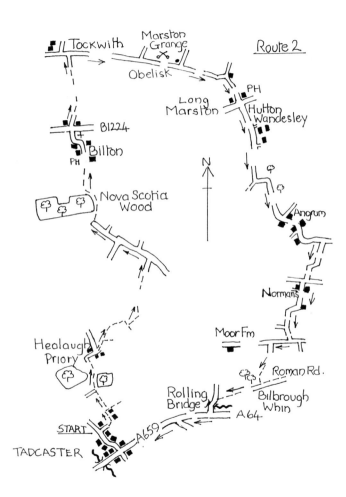

2

Route 2

Tockwith

Marston Grange

Obelisk

Long Marston

PH

Hutton Wandesley

B1224

Bilton

PH

Nova Scotia Wood

N

Angrum

Normans

Moor Fm

Healaugh Priory

Roman Rd.

Rolling Bridge

Bilbrough Whin

A64

START

A659

TADCASTER

Route : 2   TADCASTER - NOVA SCOTIA LOOP.

Distance: 15 miles; off road 17.5 miles; on road 7.5 miles
Time: 2.5 to 3 hours
Grade: 1/1
Terrain: Flat farm land, undulating open countryside.
Surface: Hard-pack tracks, quite tarmac lanes and roads.
Maps: OS Map York Sheet 105 Landranger Series.

This is probably the easiest ride in the book. Right from the start it follows hard-pack bridleways and takes in a number of quaint and historic villages. The route takes its name from the woodlands called Nova Scotia on the outskirts of Bilton. Many of the place names, such as Cromwell Clump, are a direct result of the 17th century Civil War. The battle of Marston Moor (see route 3) took place near Tockwith. It is flat or gently undulating for most of the route and could easily be ridden by an absolute novice. There are plenty of refreshment stops on route.

THE ROUTE.
Taking the A659 road east from Tadcaster town centre, go over the river and up the hill to the traffic lights. Turn L at the lights onto Wighill Lane. After 1/4 mile look out for a bridleway sign on the left indicating the bridleway across the road on the right. Turn R onto a narrow hard-pack lane between buildings. After 0.5 mile turn L through a green metal gate and continue SO.

At Healaugh Priory, after 1.8 mile, the track changes to tarmac. Go past the priory and SO at the J. The track becomes hard-pack again. Bear L at the next J, passing a number of wooden gates on either side of the track. After 3 miles, the track ends at a green metal gate and a TJ with a tarmac road. Turn L on the tarmac road and continue to where the road bears left. Take the road SO which is signposted BW to Bilton (on a wooden sign on the right). The BW continues across open fields to a left bend. Take care here as the track turns R into a field. There is a BW marker on a post on the right, and at first the grassy track is almost ST. Follow it as it gently climbs then drops to an open gateway between wooden posts with a BW sign on the right post. Turn L here and continue towards Nova Scotia Wood, bearing R alongside the wood, following the track as it winds its way towards Bilton.

The track changes to tarmac as you pass the Chequers Inn, on the left, just before entering Bilton village. Follow this road as it bears left then right and eventually meets an XR with the B1224 (note the quaint church on the right). Go SO, taking care as you cross the road, onto Moor Lane and continue for just over a mile to Tockwith. Turn R at the TJ with a road and follow this road past Marston Grange.

The obelisk, which commemorates the battle of Marston Moor (see route 3), can be seen on the left at the next TJ. Continue SO to Long Marston and then on to Hutton Wandesley. The road now continues, winding its way through Angram. As the road bears left look out for the TJ on the right and turn down this lane until you get to an offset XR. Go R them immediately L passing buildings called Normans and continue to follow the road to a TJ where you should turn R and soon afterwards turn L onto a narrow lane leading to a TJ with a bridleway at GR 522452, which leads to Bilbrough Whin. Here the track meets the old Roman road (now a grassy bridle track). Turn R along the BW through an avenue of trees and continue following this track for just over a mile to a TJ with a road. Turn L over Rolling Bridge at GR 506444 and continue to the TJ with the A64 trunk road. Turn R **and take care because of heavy traffic**. It is advisable to walk the short distance to the A659 back to the traffic lights at the XR in Tadcaster. Turn R back to the start of the route.

The Ouse bridleway near Upper Poppleton

3

Route 3.

River Ouse

Caravan Site

Moor
Monkton

Red House
School

Scagglethorpe
Moor

Thickpenny
Farm

Moor Monkton
Moor

A59

N

Upper
Poppleton

PH

Low Moor

Hall

Start
Rufforth

† PH

Airfield

Route : 3   SCAGGLETHORPE MOOR - LOW MOOR - OUSE BRIDLEWAY

Distance	13.5 miles; off road 7 miles; on road 6.5 Miles
Time	2 hours to 2 hours 30 mins.
Grade	2/2
Terrain	Riverside grassy stretches, farmland, open country side.
Surface	Tarmac-surfaced lanes and roads, Bridleways, grassy single tracks, farm tracks, all rideable.
Maps	OS map Sheet 105 Landranger series.

This is one of those pleasant rides which can be accomplished quite easily on a summer Sunday afternoon. It also makes an ideal full-day family ride with a good one third of the route following the River Ouse BW track. There are few areas which would be affected by adverse weather conditions, with the exception of one BW track, which could be muddy for about 50 yards in wet weather.

THE ROUTE.
There are a number of good starting points around the route. I have chosen to start from the village of Rufforth, GR 528515, near the spired church.

Travelling north of the village, there are two options; a) Follow the BW across the fields on the left for about a mile, until you come to a J opposite Rufforth Hall, or ; b) carry on along the road until you arrive at the same Hall. Whichever route you choose, turn R at the J shortly after the Hall, and continue SO to the next TJ and turn L. Follow the winding road for 1/2 mile to another J coming in acutely from the right.

If you pause for while at this point and look NW towards Marston Moor, it was here, in 1644, during one of the Civil War battles of the English Revolution, that Cromwell's army of Roundheads, defeated Charles 1st's Royalists, with much loss of life by both armies.

History lesson over. Turn R and follow the road over the level cross-ing and to the XR at Moor Monkton Moor. Take care crossing this busy main road (A59) and carry SO for 1/3 mile, to a road coming in from the right. Look out for a large sign for Red House School at the beginning of this road. Follow this road as it passes a YWA filtration plant on the right, and as the road bears left, a small cot-tage comes into view on the left. A BW on the right leads to Thickpenny Farm, but you need the track immediately after the cottage on the L. The route is barred by a gate, go through and follow the rather indistinct track as it crosses the fields. Fortunately there are helpful BW signs which must be followed at all times. The grassy track eventually emerges onto a tarmac road at Monkton Village. Look for a gate on the right with a sign referring to fishing rights. Go R through this gate and follow the track as it heads to-wards a caravan site. As the track bears right, carry on the less obvious track to the L towards the River Nidd. Pass through the two gates of a sheep pan, and head for the river bank and the conflu-ence of the Nidd and the Ouse. At this point, the view is worth noting as you look across the Ouse towards Beningbrough Park and the Hall. The next 3.5 miles of ST is alongside the river, with only a slight detour to avoid a water filtration unit. The track contin-ues its scenic route to Nether Poppleton.

This is a suitable stopping point for refreshments. If you con-tinue L along the road, you will come to the Lord Nelson pub. Alter-natively you can continue R through Upper Poppleton towards the station and over the level crossing which takes you up to the XR with the A59. Turn R and almost immediately L, past a large Gar-den Centre. Continue along this road until, after about one mile the surface deteriorates just as the route turns sharp R. The track gradu-ally gets narrower and becomes ST as it winds through some trees. The next 50 yards can be very rough, the surface has been broken up due to over use. The track eventually emerges into a layby along-side a road. Turn R and follow this road for just over a mile, and you will arrive back at your starting point in the village of Rufforth.

Cycle track near Naburn Wood

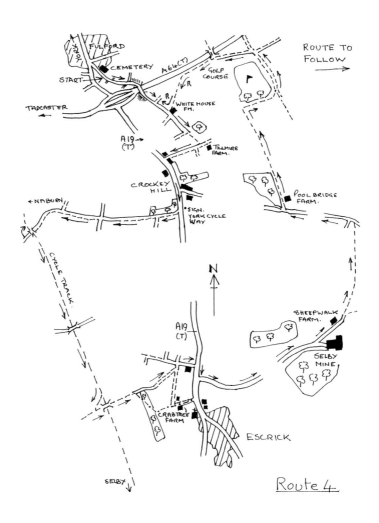

4

ROUTE TO FOLLOW →

Route 4.

Route 4   CROCKEY HILL - ESCRICK.

Distance	14 miles; off road 9.75 miles; on road 4.25 miles
Time	1 hour 30 mins to 2 hours
Grade	1/2
Terrain	Flat farm land, some rough pasture, open country side and woodland.
Surface	The majority of tracks are hard-packed dirt or rough pasture. The rest are tarmac-surfaced or cycle way.
Maps	OS map York Sheet 105 Landranger.

For the novice or inexperienced rider, this route provides an opportunity to get to grips with off-road riding, without the problems often encountered on more technical routes. The whole route is relatively flat; only in very wet conditions would some of the farm track become muddy, but then only for short distances. The picturesque villages and wooded copse seem to add to the quiet serenity of this area, and make this an ideal ride for a family group.

THE ROUTE
From York, take the A19 trunk road S. At Fulford village, take the Fordham road on the L heading towards the cemetery. Follow this road through a small estate until the road surface changes to a dirt track and it becomes a BW. The track goes SO over the A64 trunk road via a narrow bridge. Soon after a track comes in from the left, ignore this, and continue on to White House Farm. Go SO for 1/4 mile until the track turns right. Again, ignore the turn and carry SO towards Tillmire Farm and a TJ. Turn R and follow the track as it comes to another TJ with the A19 road.

   This is a very busy stretch of road and care should be taken as you turn L and follow it for a short distance to Crockey Hill. Look out for a long red brick wall on your right as you ride through this small hamlet. As the wall turns to the right down a lane, you will notice a signpost, by the roadside, pointing towards Naburn and the York

Cycle Way. Follow this route as it takes you along a narrow lane between woods and then opens out onto a long straight stretch of road. After 1.5 miles, a bridge crosses the road and you must take a turn R up a narrow track in order to get onto the York Cycle Way.

The cycle-way was created from a railway track which previously ran from York to Selby. Sustrans, a civil engineering charity, is developing a number of these old rail tracks, turning them into leisure routes for walkers and cyclists. This particular route provides access to several alternative routes on either side of the track.

Once on the cycle track, head S towards Selby. Look out for walkers on this track, many with young children or dogs. **Give way to them or slow down as you pass by**.

You should now be looking for two bridges crossing over the cycle way. Carry on under the first one, then a mile further on you will come to the second bridge. Turn off the track to the R and then go over the bridge to the L, onto a rough track leading down past some oak trees on the left. The track gradually improves and after a 1/4 of a mile it divides, the right track becoming a RUPP and leading directly down to Crabtree Farm (but it is not the best track). You must continue SO on the BW, heading towards a collection of buildings called Deighton. This track ends at the TJ with the A19 trunk road. Turn R on the A19. Take care this is a busy road. (If you followed the RUPP down to Crabtree Farm you will have to turn L at the J with the A19 main road). Continue on the road for a short stretch to a signpost indicating Selby Mine, turn L down this road. Again exercise caution; this is a busy site access road used by heavy lorries during the week, and although it is wide you will need to take **care**. Follow this road for one mile to where the road bends to the right. Just on the bend and before the mine entrance, look for a narrow lane which leads off to the L, going down to Sheepwalk Farm. Carry on past the farm, following the waymarked signs on the L of Warren House Farm; this track may become quite muddy in wet weather. Carry SO to a TJ with a classified road.

At this junction it may be possible to take a short detour to Wheldrake Village, where there are shops and a public house if you need refreshment. To get to the village go R at this TJ, (It's about a mile down the road). If you prefer to continue with the route, go L and carry on down the road for just over one mile, to where the road narrows at a bridge on a bend. Be careful as you cross the road to reach the BW on the R leading on to Poole Bridge Farm. As you pass the farm, which is on the right, the track becomes more like a grassy avenue between rows of trees. In summer this field is used as a caravan site, but further along, and perhaps more worthy of attention, are the red signs which **warn you of bulls** ! I must admit, I saw nothing more alarming than a stoat, which ran out across my path. But nevertheless, be warned !

Continue along this rough pathway, passing through two gates. At the second gate go R, following the BW signs onto a ST through a strip of woodland, which passes close to a golf course on the left. At the right time of year, you will be treated to an amazing scene - the ground is smothered with huge Fly Agaric Toadstools. These brightly coloured red and white spotted fungi are extremely poisonous. **Do not attempt to touch them**: even the smallest ingested amounts can cause nausea and even unconsciousness.

If you have not turned back by now, carry on through the wooded area to a clearing and a wider track. Turn L. This is Heslington Common, parts of which are now a golf course. Carry on across the Common, following the track for 1/2 mile to a TJ with another track. Go L - you can see the A64 trunk road on your right, running parallel to the track you are on. Continue on the track until you come to a narrow bridge which crosses the A64. Do not cross the bridge, but follow the waymarked signs SO on a ST around a slight overgrown area. Follow this track close to the main road as it bears L near a wooded area, eventually emerging at White House Farm which you passed at the start of your ride. Turn R at the farm and head back over the A64 via the bridge, to your starting point.

5

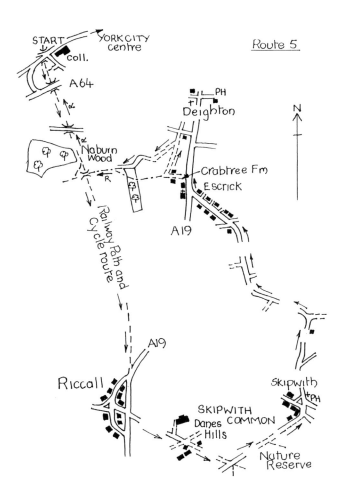

Route 5

Route : 5   YORK CYCLE-WAY - RICCALL - SKIPWITH COMMON.

Distance:	19.5 miles; off road 14 miles; on road 5.5 miles.
Time:	2 to 3 hours at a leisurely pace.
Grade:	1/2
Terrain:	Flat open countryside, wooded Nature Reserve, no real hills.
Surface:	Hard-pack converted railtrack (Sustrans), roughish track through Nature Reserve
Maps:	OS Map York Sheet 105 Landranger Series.

This is one of those rides that you tend to reserve for a family outing, or perhaps a leisurely summer's evening jaunt if you live within reasonable distance. However, there are always those days in winter, when you need a steady ride, without having to burn up too much energy, this route should be ideal for that purpose.

Using the Sustrans converted railtrack, which now links the City of York to Selby, it is possible to head off at a number of suitable points along the track, in order to sample the delights of the countryside of the area. The Skipwith Nature Reserve offers you the opportunity to ride through a quiet woodland, undisturbed by traffic noise, and maybe even spot some of the rather rarer species of wildlife which can be found here.

THE ROUTE.
The start point, GR581485, is just off the A1036 road shortly after the intersection with the A64. It is signposted as a Cycle Route and starts just across the road from York 6th Form College by the traffic lights.

The route initially starts off as the Selby - Middlethorpe cycle track, but as it enters a new housing area, follow the sign to Selby. The short excursion round the houses, soon brings you back to the track. The surface is crushed stone, rolled flat. When dry it can be quite dusty, but when wet, it seems fairly well drained, with the occasional puddle to navigate. Follow the track for the next 6 miles, heading S for Riccall. The railtrack ends here, so turn R into Riccall village and follow the road as it bears left and comes to a XR by a church. Turn L and follow this road for a short distance to a TJ with the A19 (York - Selby road). Cross this road, taking care as you do so, it is a very busy road, and almost immediately, turn L down King Rudding Lane. Follow this lane for just over a mile to where it enters Skipwith Common Nature Reserve.

As the road enters the woods, it deteriorates and becomes a very bumpy track, with broken tarmac and pot-holes. This is more than made up for, because the scenery is quite rewarding, with an avenue of Oak, Birch and Ash trees to ride through. (The area is noted for its wild life. Particularly migrating birds, which come to nest here each year).

Just before the village of Skipwith, the track divides, bear L and ride on to the village green. There is a pub here if you need refreshment. From the pub, head N along the road to Escrick. Do not turn off, carry on to Escrick village, where you come to a TJ with the A19, just opposite a church and a hotel.

Turn R along the A19, again take care as you cross the road. Look out for the sign to Crabtree Farm on the left, which appears, soon after you have crossed the road. Go L down this track towards the farm and continue to where it turns sharp R just after the farm. (There is a RUPP which goes straight across the field ahead, but it is not advisable). Go R and follow the track for 0.3 mile to where a track comes in acutely from the left. Turn L here and head back, almost in the direction you have come, making for a small wooded area, which you skirt round, before climbing up onto a redbrick bridge which spans the cycle track you rode down earlier. Cross over the bridge, and descend to the track below, by turning R through an opening in the wooden fence. Once on the track, head N towards York, and back to the starting point, just over 3 miles away.

The tree-lined route through Skipwith Common.

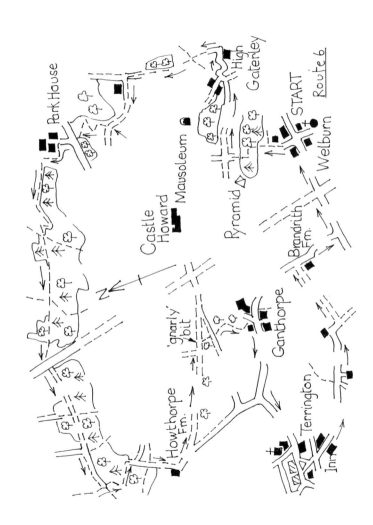

6

Route 6

START

Welburn

High Gatenley

Park House

Mausoleum

Castle Howard

Pyramid

Brandrith Fm.

Ganthorpe

'gnarly' bit

Howthorpe Fm.

Terrington

Inn

Route 6 WELBURN - CASTLE HOWARD.

Distance	17 miles; off road 13.75 miles; on road 3.25 miles.
Time	2 hours 45 mins to 3 hours 30 mins.
Grade	3/3 This could change either way depending on weather conditions.
Terrain	Varying, from flat woodland, to undulating fields, some areas may become very muddy after heavy rain, but only in short stretches.
Surface	Some tarmac road, good hard-pack farm tracks, forest tracks, some single tracks.
Maps	OS Map Malton & Pickering Sheet 100 Landranger Series

This route uses some of the trails which surround Castle Howard grounds. It is in a beautiful setting, which varies from mixed woodland, to open farm land, changing frequently as you ride. For those who enjoy the distinctive smell of pine forest, mingled with the equally distinctive smell of arable farm land, this is the ride for you.

In total, it is not too difficult, but there are sections that could be difficult for the novice rider. These sections are short enough to be walked, if you do not feel too confident about riding them. For the experienced rider, the gnarly downhill runs and the testing short grassy climbs, will make the ride a promising one.

THE ROUTE.
Starting from Welburn village, GR 722680, go down Water Lane and follow the road as it becomes a ST leading across a field to a gate into a wood known as East Moor Banks. The track bears L as it goes down and then up again, to exit the wood by a gate.

Crossing the field, you will see on your left, a structure known as the Pyramid. As the track meets a TJ, go R on a surfaced track, passing another curious domed building called the Mausoleum, set back on the left and just appearing above the trees. Continue SO to a farm at Low Gaterley. Just as you reach the farm, take the track to the R where a painted sign points to High Gaterley.

The track dips then climbs up a hill passing fields on either side, where you may see dozens of Shetland Ponies. Continue on to the farm and shortly after, turn L down a track leading to Easthorpe Hall stud farm. As you reach the farm, the track divides. Go L through the farm, but watch out for geese ! The track continues E and as it bends to the R, look out for a rough indistinct ST crossing a short grassy stretch, and leading to a wooden gate in a fence by the wood. Go through this gate and into a field. The track here is hard to distinguish, but follow some old track markings up a steep grassy slope, bearing R then sharp L as you near the top of the hill. You should be able to see the gateway across the field to the L leading onto the road. Cross the road to Park House and follow the track until you reach the farm. Do not go through the farm, but bear L on the lower side of a barn, then R up to a gate. The next part of the route is flattish for at least 2 miles; it can also be muddy in places. Follow the track, which varies in places from ST to forest track, as it continues to the right of Coneysthorpe Banks Wood. Ignore any tracks coming in from the left or the right, until you come to a gate leading into a field. Here you have a fine view of the valley just below. Ride down the fast descent to a gate and a TJ with a road.

Cross the road and go up the track into Slingsby Banks Wood. The track continues along the top side of the wood, passing a BW from the right, which goes down to Slingsby Village and the possibility of refreshments if needed. If not go SO and continue SO at the next XR and again SO, passing the track coming in on the right from Fryton village, until just over 1/2 mile you meet a XR with BW signs. Go L and follow the ST which is quite rough at first, as it descends through woods to a gate. Go through and up to an open field. Bear R and follow the track up to Howthorpe Farm. As the track comes up to the farm, it bears L by an ancient dome-shaped stone pillar in the ground. Follow the BW signs along the hard packed surface for 3/4 mile to where the track divides. Follow the track up to the L, continue alongside the woods on your right and as you enter Bell Bottom wood, you pass a track on the left but continue SO to a steeply descending ST on your R. Take care as you follow this slippery ST over exposed roots, down to a road.

At this point in the journey, if you feel that you need a break and something to eat and drink, go down to your R, and follow the road which takes you into Terrington Village and a number of hostelries which serve refreshments. (You can pick up the route again in the village, just follow the directions given later, from Terrington.*)

If you intend to continue, cross the road and follow the BW sign pointing to a ST running alongside Cum Hag Wood with fields on the right. This is a rough, undefined pathway and difficult to negotiate in places. The track widens as it climbs to a farm in Ganthorpe Village. Go through the farm and onto the road at a TJ. Turn R and follow the road as it descends and then climbs up to Terrington Village.* If you stopped at the Bay Horse pub earlier, you can join the route again from here.

From the village, go L at a triangular junction and follow the track as it goes on past a cemetery on the right, and continues on to Mowthorpe, a collection of farm buildings at the top of a rise. Carry SO, and as one descends down a stone-slabbed track to another building, go R through a gate and then immediately L alongside a small lake. Stay on this track as it climbs, steeply at first, then levelling off as it reaches Brandrith Farm and a TJ with a road. Go R and follow the road to a TJ with another road coming from Bulmer Village. Turn L and follow the road down to Welburn and the start point.

The Obelisk marking the site of the Battle of Marston Moor in 1644.

In the woodland near Castle Howard.

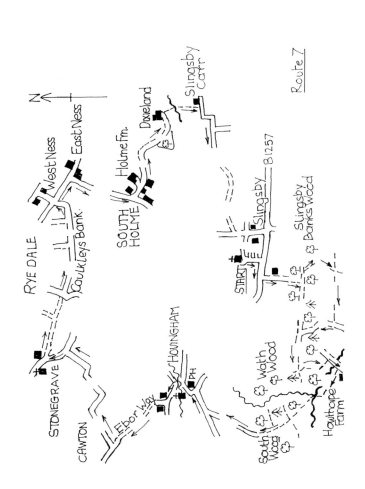

Route 7

Route 7   SLINGSBY - CAULKLEY'S BANK - BARTON MOOR.

Distance	15 miles; off road 12 miles; on road 3 miles.
Time	3 hours
Grade	2/3 Wet conditions will affect this grade, making it more difficult to negotiate some of the tracks, a 3/4 grade would then be appropriate
Terrain	Woodland, undulating arable land, open farm land, panoramic views from two high Banks, some tracks could be muddy in wet weather.
Surface	Hard, well-surfaced BW's, forest trails, single track, rough farm tracks, grass tracks and unclassified roads.
Maps	OS Map Sheet 100 Landranger Series.

This route offers the double bonus of fine views across the Vale of York to the south from the top of Slingsby Banks, and an even more panoramic scene from the top of Caulkley's Bank which over-looks Rye Dale to the north, and the Barton Moors to the east. Again, the trail takes you just north of the Castle Howard estate into a time-warped situation where everywhere seems to have retained strong links with a more serene and bygone age.

Although the route is relatively flat in places, there are a number of testing little climbs and one longish drag up Caulkley's Bank. But the views from the top and the descents that follow, more than make up for the effort required to get there.

THE ROUTE.

Starting in Slingsby Village by the church, GR 696749, ride up High Street, passing the 17th Century ruined castle on your left until you meet a TJ. Turn R and after 200 yds. turn L at the BW signpost (leaning at a precarious angle) and continue up the track towards a farm building on the left. Carry on past the buildings to a gate, which allows entry into Slingsby Banks wood. There are two possible routes at this point, L or R, both of which lead to the same track at the top of the wood.

Taking a R turn at the gate, follow the fence on your right for a short distance, to a grassy track leading up through the pine trees on the L. Ride up this track to a TJ at the top. Turn L and follow the farm track to where another track meets it from the right. Go down this unmade track, bearing right as it descends very steeply between the trees, eventually emerging in a clearing by an open gate. Turn R through the gate following the greasy track into the open fields as it runs alongside a fence at the bottom of the wood you have just come through. Continue following this track as it passes through two gates, ignore any tracks on either side until you come to a third gate. At this X R, turn R up the wide, hard-packed track as it returns to Fryton Wood via a short but steep climb.

At the top of the climb, you look down towards the village of Fryton, which can be reached by the beckoning, fast, straight track ahead of you. No such luck! You have to turn left at this X R. Continue along the rutted track for 1/2 mile to a second, rather indistinct X R.

Turn sharp L, almost going back on yourself. Here the track becomes rougher as it heads back into the wood to descend down to a gate. Go SO to the next gate where the track may be a little muddy. A short climb brings you to a third gate and out into open fields again. Turn R, following the wide farm track as it heads towards a couple of ponds. Just after the pond on the right, turn R where a BW sign directs you along the Centenary Way. This track is not very obvious, but it follows the stream running alongside the edge of the wood on your right. After passing through two metal gates, turn R at the second gate, where the sign indicates Ebor Way (sign on fence). You are now on a rough ST, and following a fence and the stream as the track heads towards a clearing in a NE direction. Where the track meets a small wooden gate with the sign indicating Ebor and Centenary Ways, follow the Centenary sign and go through the gate and across the field to a second gate which leads into the wood just ahead.

Enter the wood through the gate and climb the forest track which takes you through South Woods. Do not turn off, remain on this track until you leave the wood down a track through a field. Where the track meets the road, turn R and head down the road into Hovingham. This is probably an ideal spot for a rest if you need one. A small bakery by the church makes excellent cakes and vegetarian snacks.

Continuing on the route. Go L by the bakery and cross the stream, either by the ford, or by the small foot bridge, continuing alongside the picturesque stream until you reach a J and a sign indicating 'Rights of Way'. Go R, follow the road between the cottages until you reach a wooden gate. Follow the BW sign Ebor Way, to the R and continue along this flat, hard-packed track for almost 2 miles, to Cawton Village. Where the track emerges at the Cawton village stone sign post, turn R onto a tarmac road. Follow this road for 1.30 mile to Stonegrave Village. As the road bears left and begins to climb up past the 8th Century Priory, look out for the BW sign up on the right as the track heads almost back on the road and climbs steeply up to Caulkley's Bank. The track is rough in places, but after passing through a gate, it begins to level off and you now have panoramic views on either side of the ridge (or Bank as it is called). When the track meets a road, go SO, but look out for traffic coming over the brow from the left by a carpark as you cross the road. The track continues to descend without turning off, eventually coming to a road at the small village of West Ness. Go R at this J and follow the road as it bears sharp R after 1/4 mile. Carry on down over the Holbeck river towards South Holme, looking out for the turning off to the L by some farm buildings. This track leads to Holme Farm and the quaintly named Dixieland.

The track is tarmac at first but changes to hard-pack after Holme Farm, which is on the left. The track bears round to the right — ignore any other tracks on either side — and continue on to Dixieland Farm. At the farm, follow the fence, which skirts around the farm to the right. Continue following the fence, which is on your left-hand side, and bear R by a waymark on the fence keeping close to the hedgerow as you make for a gap between some bushes. Here you will find a narrow gate immediately followed by another (this is a Wanglethrop barrier designed to make the travellers journey difficult). Having negotiated this obstacle, head straight up an embankment ahead of you to some waymark signs on a post. Go to the right and down the other side of the embankment heading towards a gate. The track continues through the gate following a wire fence on the right. Head for a corner of the farm just in front of you (Slingsby Carr Farm), following the hard surfaced road as it turns R then L and then R again. At a left bend in the road go SO along the grassy BW which takes you back to a TJ with a quiet road. Turn L along the road to the start point.

Bridleway from Slingsby Carr passing stacked hay bales.

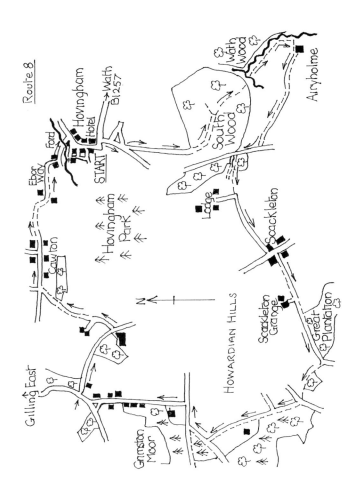

8

Route 8

Route : 8   HOVINGHAM PARK — GRIMSTON MOOR.

Distance:	11.75 miles; off road 9 miles; on road 2.75 miles.
Time:	1,75 to 2.25 hours, depending on conditions.
Grade:	2/2
Terrain:	Undulating, wooded parkland, some farmland, picturesque views from several vantage points, no steep climbs.
Surface:	Mainly bridleways and woodland tracks. Some tarmac roads, short stretch of single track.
Maps:	OS Map. Sheet 100 Landranger Series.

Hovingham Park is situated about 8 miles west of Malton near the picturesque village of Hovingham. The route is fairly easy, with only one or two slightly harder sections to contend with. This is the type of ride you can try on a summer afternoon, or for the fitter rider, link with routes 6 or 7 to make a much longer ride.

THE ROUTE.
Start from the layby, GR 667753, just south of the village of Hovingham, and follow the signposted BW up to South Wood. Go SO following the track through the wood, ignoring any turnings, until a badly placed BW sign on the right, indicates a turn off to the L. Follow this track down to a gate and a sign indicating the Ebor Way. Go through the gate and cross the short stretch of open grassland directly ahead of you, heading towards a second gate. Turn L after going through the gate and follow the BW sign which takes you through an overgrown wooded section on a ST. When the track meets a TJ, turn R and follow this track up past Airyholme Farm onto a tarmac road. Go R along this road for a short distance, then turn L onto a second BW. At this point **take care**. The route you

take is off to the left and is hidden by bushes, The other more obvious track leads to a dead end, so don't take it!

Taking the concealed ST to the L, follow it down as it twists and turns until it eventually widens and leads on to a TJ at a small community called Scackleton. Here turn L onto a tarmac road then immediately R alongside a farm building. This track leads SO to Scackleton Grange. Carry SO on a hard-pack track, which deteriorates as it passes the Grange, on the right, and head towards a woodland called the Great Plantation. The track runs along the edge of this wood. As it reaches the end of the wood, the main track begins to bear left, but look out for a rougher ST to the R. Take this track down through a wood which is ST in places and follow it until it emerges at a tarmac road. Go R then L into a wood and climb up the steep narrow track through the pine trees, passing a farm on the left at the top of the climb. The track emerges at a TJ with a tarmac road. This is Grimston Moor. Go R and follow the road for a short distance to a second TJ. Continue R, then L at the first turning. Follow this tarmac road and shortly after passing Grimston Moor Farm, you arrive at a junction with the B1363 road. Go R then take the next turn R just before Mill Wood.

Follow this flattish road for just less than a mile, to a BW on the L with quite a wide entrance. (It serves as an access road to Syke Gate Farm on the left, higher up). Follow this BW a it climbs for a short distance before descending with a fast run down to a TJ with a road. Go R along this road which takes you to Cawton Village. Go through the village and where the road bears left at the village sign (a large stone wheel set up on a plinth on a small grassy mound), go SO along the route signposted Ebor Way. This fast, flat track takes you past the old Hovingham Spa on the left before returning to Hovingham village. As you cross the ford, a welcome

A typical single track.

bakery shop greets you with a variety of vegetarian pies and food-stuffs as well as good old sticky buns, so indulge yourself ! The start point is a short distance back up the main road.

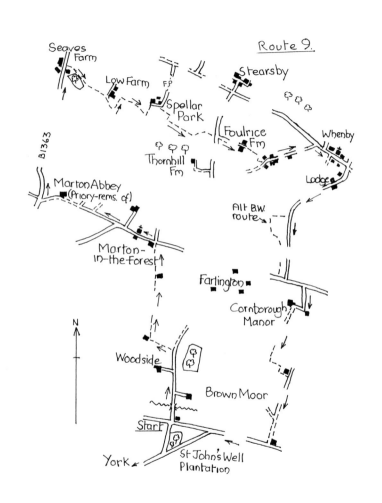

9

Route 9.

Seaves Farm
Low Farm
FP
Stearsby
Spellar Park
Foulrice Fm
Whenby
B1363
Thornhill Fm
Marton Abbey
(Priory-rems. of)
Lodge
Alt B.W. route
Marton-in-the-forest
Farlington
Cornborough Manor
N
Woodside
Brown Moor
Start
York
St John's Well Plantation

Route 9   MARTON - IN - THE - FOREST.

Distance	14 miles; off road 5.5 miles; on road 8.5 miles.
Time	2 hours in good conditions.
Grade	1/2
Terrain	Farm land, meadow land, some scattered woodland historic landmarks, mostly flat, easy riding.
Surface	Narrow tarmac lanes, hard-pack bridleways and some rough tracks. Meadow tracks are often indistinct and are followed one gate to the next.
Maps	OS Map. Sheet 100 Landranger Series.

This is an easy ride and because there are quite a number of historic sites *en-route*, it is worth taking time out to look at them, or simply enjoy the rustic simplicity of the villages. The bridleways are not a daunting prospect, but in places, where the farmer has ploughed a little bit too energetically, the track may become rough, but this is confined to short distances. It is rather annoying though, to find that some legal bridleways are being treated in this manner, spoiling what would otherwise be a clear, continuous route.

THE ROUTE.
Starting from or near St John's Well Plantation, GR 605657, on Brown Moor, ride in a northerly direction along the lane from the road junction, passing a cottage on the right. Continue along the lane until just after Woodside Farm on the left, 0.6 mile from the start, an unmarked track heads L across fields. Follow the track, bearing R at an old barn. Carry on to a farm where the track becomes rougher as it passes on the left of the farm and continues up a slight climb to a road. The BW sign appears at the exit together with a Foss Walk sign. Turn L and go along the road through Marton

village. As the road bends to the left, go SO down a narrow lane to Marton Abbey and the Priory remains. If you have time, pause a while and take in some of the historic interest of the place.

Where the lane meets the road, turn R. (It is possible to take a detour down a BW on the L, which takes you to Crayke Village and more ancient remains, about 2 miles away). If you choose to go SO, continue along the B1363 for just over a mile, and look out for Seave Farm on the left (the name of the farm appears on a garage door). Directly opposite the farm on the R is a metal gate leading onto the BW. Go through this gate and follow the track as it heads towards a wood on the right. A wooden gate leads you into the next field. Cross this field to the metal gates which appear directly ahead. At this point the blue waymarkers seem to have been removed and following the track becomes more difficult. Keeping alongside the hedgerow, continue below Low Farm, but watch out for the track becoming obscured as it turns NE towards Spellar Park Farm.

Cross the field towards the corner of the farm where you will see a wooden gateway, go through and follow the short track to a second series of metal gates. Go through the metal gate ahead of you, which leads into a field containing recently planted saplings on the left-hand side of the field. The track is not obvious but follows the line of saplings down to a gully and stays on the right-hand side of the gully. Go directly across the open field until the track emerges at a TJ with a tarmac road. (This bridle route is currently being reviewed by York Council and it is hoped that better markings and a more obvious track will be the outcome.) Cross the road and follow the bridleway to Foul Rice Farm. Go through the farm, taking care, and continue to follow the BW to a TJ. Turn R and follow the road to Whenby Village. Go through the village past the church on the left, look out for the signpost indicating Whenby Lodge. Turn R at the imposing entrance and ride down the smooth tarmac driveway, passing a cottage on the right as you traverse a cattle grid before climbing a short rise to the Bull pans. **Please take care going through the yard**, as this is a stock breeding area. Continue along the lane until you reach the BW sign on the right. This route is badly over-ploughed in places and is not worth the struggle unless you really want to. It is easier to continue along the lane to a TJ with a road. At the farm, turn L for a short distance, looking out foe a sign to Cornbrough Manor on the right.

This is probably a good point to make a detour to see Sheriff Hutton Castle (remains), about 2 miles along the road. If not, return to the route and turn R to Cornbrough Manor. The track heads towards an electric power relay station, which seems totally incongruous in its surroundings. As the track skirts around the station, turn R and head towards the Manor house. Just before the house, go through a gate on the L and ride down the track to a second gate. Continue down the track until you appear to be stopped by a hedge directly in front of you. The track now turns L and becomes rough for about 50 yds, as it follows the hedge to a small gateway. Go through the gate and continue L across a field to another gate. Again go through this gate and once more the track becomes rough as you follow it up to the road. Turn R t the road, you are now back at Brown Moor. A short ride to the main road junction and a right turn will take you back to your starting point.

The bridleway near Marton-in-the-Forest.

A typical Wolds pub.

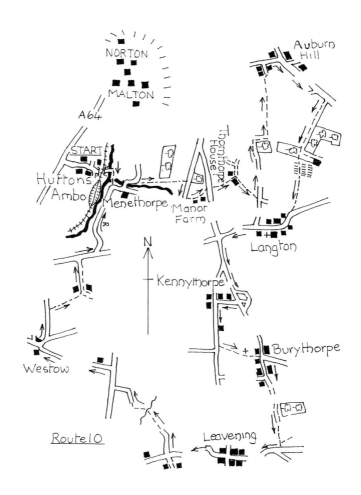

10

NORTON

MALTON

A64

START

Huttons
Ambo

Menethorpe

Thornthorpe House

Manor Farm

Auburn Hill

Langton

N

Kennythorpe

Burythorpe

Westow

Leavening

Route 10

Route 10   THE BECKS CIRCLE.

Distance	14 miles; off road 8.5 miles; on road 5.5 miles.
Time	2 to 3 hours depending on conditions.
Grade	2/3
Terrain	Undulating open farm land, woodland and short steep climbs — typical Wolds countryside.
Surface	Smooth tarmac lanes, hard-pack BWs, farm tracks & grassy single tracks, well drained in most areas.
Maps	OS Map Sheet 100 Landranger Series.

The land just south of Malton and Norton seems to be the catchment area for all the becks which run into the River Derwent from Birdsall Brow Ridge. As a result, the land is divided by a series of ridges and troughs, running from SE to NW, creating an interesting and varied landscape. The quiet country lanes link grassy bridle tracks to short steep climbs past historic sites and tiny villages full of character.

THE ROUTE.
From the start just after the railway bridge in Huttons Ambo, GR 764676, follow the suspended foot bridge over the River Derwent and onto a small track which brings you out at a road. Go L and follow the road as it heads towards Menethorpe. Shortly after crossing the bridge, the road bends to the R and on the corner is a gate on the right which leads onto a BW. Go through the gate and follow the grassy track across the field as it runs alongside the beck, eventually emerging on to a road. Go R then L after 100 yds, onto a BW which passes Manor Farm on the lower side and soon after comes to a road. Cross over the road and take the track directly ahead into a field. This track divides after a short distance. Take the L

track through the gate, following the rough track at the side of the field which leads to Thornthorpe House. Turn R at the back of the barn (look for the waymark sign on a tree), go through a gate and make your way down through the field. The track is not well defined, but head towards a gate at the bottom corner of the field on the left. Go through the gate and continue along the track in the direction of Langton Village. At a TJ with a track running N and S, turn L and follow this wider track as it first drops, then climbs up a steep slope alongside a wood on the right.

At the top of the hill, Langton Wold, turn R and follow the track as it keeps to the edge of the wood and then turns sharp left at a fence where there is a BW sign which leads off down a narrow track through fields keeping close to a hedge on the right. As the track reaches a point where it begins to climb, watch out for where it suddenly turns R through the hedge and drops steeply down for a short distance before you have to dismount and climb a few steps which lead onto a road with houses on either side. Follow this road to a TJ and turn R down the road that leads you to a XR. Go R (road sign to Birdsall) and climb Auburn Hill for 3/4 mile. Look out for the BW sign on the R which takes you onto a track past the Tree Dykes, some ancient earthworks. Continue up this track to West Wold Farm and go through the small wood straight ahead.

At the gate, exit the wood and go SO down between the tumuli banks to a second gate. Go through this gate and the track takes you straight down to the road leading to Langton Village. Where the track meets the road, turn R and follow the road in a westerly direction through the village for just less than a mile, until you reach a XR. Turn L towards Burythorpe, but where the road divides, bear L towards Kennythorpe. Just before the end of the village, opposite a grassy triangular patch of land, turn R up a lane. At a TJ, turn L onto a road and follow it for 1/2 mile. Shortly after passing a water-pumping house, take the BW on the L which climbs up to Burythorpe Church which looks as though it's in the middle of a field. When you reach the church, you will see that it is in a field !

Take the tarmac lane SO down to Burythorpe Village and turn R at the TJ. Follow the road for 1/4 mile, passing a pub on the left, then where the road bends to the right, look for the sign indicating route not suitable for vehicles. Go SO down this lane past farm buildings on the right, through the gates, onto a deteriorating track which eventually brings you to a steep uphill climb. The way forward is through a gate which leads onto an avenue of bushes and trees. It is overgrown in places, but there has been an attempt to lay a hard-core surface at sometime in the past, which makes riding a little easier.

For those of you interested in local history, there are the remains of a Motte and Bailey over to the left of the track you are climbing, but not much is known about it.

The track ends abruptly at a gate and becomes less obvious as it enters a field littered with hawthorn bushes. Keep going SO up the hill, looking for evidence of the track, which appears in short stretches between the bushes. At the top of the climb, a gate bars the way onto a road. Go through the gate and turn R downhill on the road - a welcome relief after the climb. At the village of Leavening, continue SO past the Jolly Farmer pub, up the hill to a sign on the left indicating Clifton Farm, and take the wide gravel track on the R. Follow this good ST for a mile. On reaching a TJ with a road, turn R then almost immediately L up a track which passes Westow Low Grange where the going becomes harder as it gets more overgrown in places. Where the track emerges at a road, turn R then L onto a road signposted 'Church Only'. Follow this road SO past a pumping station on the right and soon after the BW sign appears on the R. Follow this rough track at the side of the field to Grange

Farm. Turn L through the farm yard, passing an ancient railway carriage on the right next to two silos. Continue down the farm track to a TJ with a road. Turn R along this road and after 300 yds., turn L up the road to Menethorpe. Look out for the narrow entrance to the pathway you came along at the beginning of the ride - it will be on your L and signposted Centenary Way. Go back over the suspension bridge, and to the start in Huttons Ambo.

Byland Abbey

There's a BW somewhere ! The Wolds Way route to Warrendale Farm.

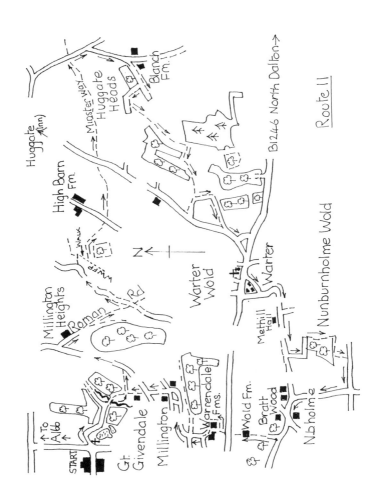

11

Huggate (Inn)

Musterway

Huggate Heads

Blanch Fm.

B1246 North Dalton →

High Barn Fm.

N ←

Warter Wold

Warter

Nunburnholme Wold

Millington Heights

Roman

WYFR

Millington Rd

Methill Hall

Gt. Givendale

Millington

Warrendale Fms.

Wold Fm.

Bratt Wood

N.bholme

← To A166

START

Route 11

Route 11 GIVENDALE - WARTER WOLD - HUGGATE HEADS.

Distance:	24 miles; off road 15.5 miles; on road 8.5 miles
Time:	3 hours 30 mins to 4 hours.
Grade:	3/3
Terrain:	Woodland, open farm land, undulating hills-valleys-hill; typical Wolds country
Surface:	Tarmac lanes, bridleways, single track, grass tracks.
Maps:	OS Map, Sheet 106 Landranger Series.

The Yorkshire Wolds provide a relatively untapped area for off-road routes of outstanding beauty and interest. The numerous hills and valleys, constantly screen what lies ahead. Each hill climbed, leads to a new hidden valley, with its own picturesque hamlet and the inevitable stream. The landscape is somewhat softer then the North Yorkshire Moors, but it is still sufficiently challenging.

THE ROUTE.
Givendale Village is situated just south of the A166, York-Bridlington road, near Pocklington. From the start, GR 813538, St. Ethelberga's Church, go down the BW opposite the TJ. Follow the BW as it passes a small lake on the right and go through the gate. Continue SO down the valley to a second gate, go through and climb the steep track alongside the wall where you have to negotiate an over-hanging tree branch across the path. At the top of the climb, go SO across the field to a gate leading to a road. Turn L and after 0.7 mile turn R at a BW leading to Millington Heights. Continue down through the fields on this old Roman road, going through several gates until you reach a road at TJ. Turn L and follow the narrow tarmac lane as it winds through the steep-sided valley for 0.8 mile. Where the lane bears left, there is a gate on the right and waymarked signs

(GR 850542). Go through the gate and turn R. **You are now on a short stretch of the Wolds Way footpath, so get off and walk** up the track for about 50 yds: it is steep and rough and leads to a BW sign (GR 859540) by a line of trees running in a straight line across the fields to the left. Negotiating this badly defined ST is not easy as it climbs up through the field alongside the row of trees with overhanging boughs. The track begins to bear R as it heads towards a gateway at the top of the field. Follow the direction of the Minster Way sign and go L, on the track leading to a road. Go SO across the road and continue down the BW to a second road.

At this point, you can either go straight across the road and continue along the Minster Way BW, or go L up the road for 3/4 mile to Huggate Village for refreshments at the Wolds Inn. The landlord regularly plays host to a well-known Dutch cycle racing team, which trains in this area!

If you choose to carry on across the road, follow the BW, which can be obscured by long grass at certain times of the year. At a TJ with a road, go R down the road for 1/4 mile to a BW on the R, leading to Blanch Farm. The surface is smooth as the track heads down to the farm, but watch out for the BW signs on a post on the right as you enter the farm. Bear R onto a rough track alongside a wood and follow the track as it turns R again and then bears L and starts to follow a ST along the top of a steep-sided valley.

Follow this path for 3/4 mile, and as it descends, look out for the BW sign on a post, indicating the sharp R change of direction, by turning down the grassy trackless slope into the valley bottom and SO up a steep climb on the other side to a gate. Go through the gate and follow the track to the edge of Ringlands Plantation.

A meeting of several tracks here, calls for caution. Bear L then R and carry SO, following the track to a junction just before a road. Bear L at the junction and follow the track as it bends round to the R and join the road. Go L down the fast descent to Warter Village.

At a TJ, go R, and pass the quaint village duck pond on your right just before the church. Opposite the church, turn L and climb the road to a TJ where you turn L and continue following this winding road as it climbs past Methill Hall on the right.

Soon after the Hall, look out for a BW going off to the L and climbing up a narrow ST which takes you over Nunburnholme Wold. Stay on the track as it bears left and follows the edge of a wood, eventually emerging at a road. Go R along the road to a XR, turn R and go down the steep descent into Nunburnholme Village. Follow the road through the village, bearing R at the TJ and shortly after turning R onto a BW which climbs up through Bratt Wood to a clearing where the track becomes obscure. Follow the hedgerow SO and head for Wold Farm about 1/2 mile ahead. Take care going through the farmyard, bear L, SO, then R and L to a TJ with a road. Cross the road to the Wolds Way sign, go through the gate and onto a grassy track which heads down to the corner of a wood and then follows a narrow track along the edge of a cereal crop field. It is possible that this track may become obscured by the cereal crop overhanging the path in places, but go SO the track is there ! Use the hedgerow on the left as a guide - it follows the track to Warrendale Farm. On entering the farm, **please dismount and walk through**. The track bears R, round the barns then L before leaving the farm on a tarmac road. Follow the road for 1 mile, to Millington Village. Go through the village, following the road as it bears L and climbs up to a TJ. Go across the road to the BW which takes you past Little Givendale Farm to a junction at a gate. You should recognise this point, since you turned up the track to the right earlier in the day. Go through the gate and down the steep slope by the wall on the right to the gate (watch out for the overhanging branch on your descent).

You can now retrace the route back to the church and the start point in Givendale.

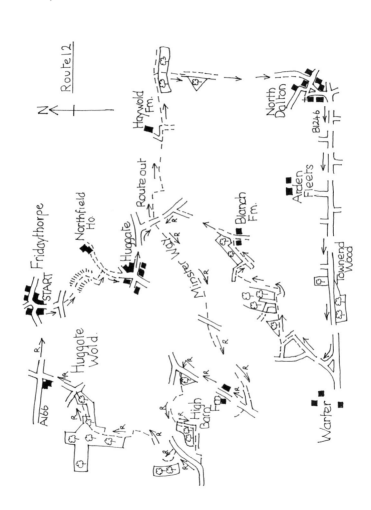

12

Route 12

Route 12.   FRIDAYTHORPE - HUGGATE HEADS - NORTH DALTON

Distance	23 miles; off road 15 miles; on road 8 miles.
Time	3 to 4 hours.
Grade	3/3
Terrain	Undulating open farm land, wooded valleys, steep-sided earthworks.
Surface	Smooth tarmac lanes, hard-pack bridleways, grassy indistinct tracks, single tracks.
Maps	OS Map Sheet 106 Landranger Series.

This is another area of the Wolds region which is steeped in Saxon and Nordic history: small villages hidden away in secluded valleys, with names reflecting their ancestry; steep-sided, massively built earthworms and fortifications of a bygone age; all contrast with the mellow woodlands and pastures. Cutting through all of this there are the bridleway systems of the Wolds and Minster Ways, heading north/south and east/west respectively.

THE ROUTE.
Starting from Fridaythorpe, GR874589, take the BW which is close to a public telephone, and heads due S. At a TJ, go SO a short distance to a gate on the L. Go through the gate and turn R, following the smooth grassy track along a valley formed by two high banked earthworks on either side. On reaching a second gate, go through and turn R, by a sign post to the Wolds Way. The ST gradually climbs up the side of an earthworks, then at the top, go through a gate and into a field. Cross the field to another gate which leads onto the tarmac lane coming from Northfield House.

This lane gradually leads you into Huggate village, past the quaintly named Sam Suddaby Farm Church. At the X Rd., turn R past the Wolds Inn on your left, and carry on until you reach a junction. Take the R fork and after 1.25 mls, turn L on the Minster Way, heading E. Continue along this grassy track for about 1 1/2 miles where the surface changes to a hard-pack surface and then bears left back onto the BW again, heading down through fields to a wood. Go through two wooden gates into the woods on the R. Follow the BW signs along a ST through the wood and up a steep but short climb which enters a field at the top. Still following the BW sign, go across the field to where the track becomes a long, fast, straight descent to North Dalton Village. This is an ideal place for a refreshment stop. There are a number of places serving food and drink in this pleasant little village.

After the descent down the BW into the village, you arrive at a TJ with the B 1246 road . Turn R and follow the road through North Dalton, heading W towards Warter Village. Continue along this road for 4 miles (unfortunately a possible off-road route via Blanch Farm, is not possible, part of the route being a footpath, despite requests to change its status). Shortly before Warter, just after Townend Wood on your left, look out for the turning on the R. Go up this road, bearing R at a junction and then R again onto a BW soon after. Follow this BW as it turns a sharp L and, after 1/4 mile, turn sharp R just before the BW you are on, heads back to the road.

Continue along this BW, heading almost E, passing first one wood, then as you pass the end of a second wood, the track arrives at a junction with another track on the left. Ignore this track and look for the ST which goes SO down alongside a wood on the left and a fence on the right. Go through the gate and then the track drops suddenly down a steep descent to a valley floor. Go SO across the valley floor and up the bank to a wooden signpost on the other side. (The track does not show well at this point). At the post, turn L up the hill and follow the line of the valley and the woods below on your left as you dodge in and out of the Hawthorn trees on the narrow ST. The track eventually widens as it bears R then L as it passes through a wood near Blanch Farm. Follow the track to the farm where a BW sign on a telegraph pole indicates the way. Carry on heading N E up the tarmac lane until you reach a TJ with a road, go L on this road for 1/4 mile and look out for a BW on the L (Minster Way).

This BW takes you across Huggate Heads, an open expanse of fields. The track crosses one road, then at the second road, turn R, heading towards High Barn Farm. Continue past the farm until you reach a small wooded area on the left. At the end of this wood, just before a TJ, look out for a partially hidden BW sign on the L. Go along this rough track as it crosses fields above a valley below on the right. After 1/2 mile the track bears R and then circles round to the L to meet a small wood. At the corner of this wood, go through the gate and onto the track leading through the top side of the wood. At a second gate, go R and follow a fast track down to a point where it turns sharp L. Take care as you descend this loose-surfaced track, which takes you down to a gate on the R and onto the valley road.

Turn R and follow the road for 1/4 mile then turn L at the BW sign which directs you into a field and an indistinct track which follows the valley bottom, (evidence of more earthworks on the right). Eventually the track turns L up the valley to a wood on the left which it runs alongside for nearly 1/2 mile before going into the wood and bearing R. Then keep R as the track divides when it climbs out of the wood and meets a road at a TJ. Go SO past some large stone posts by the road side and eventually you meet the A166 at a TJ . Take care as you cross this busy road and turn R to follow the road back to Fridaythorpe.

The track from Fridaythorpe between the huge earthworks.

Bridleway leading down to Mount Ferrant.

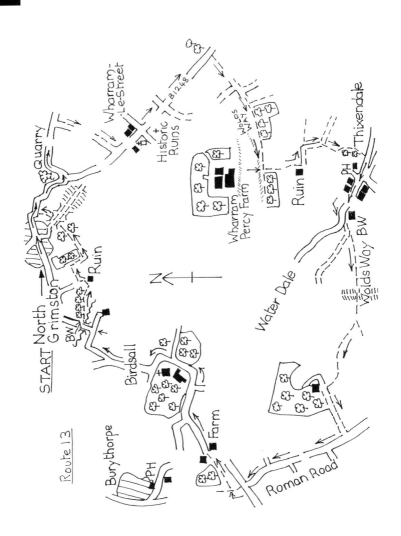

13

Route 13

START North Grimston

Quarry

Wharram-le-Street

Historic Ruins

B1248

Wolds Way

Wharram Percy Farm

Ruin

PH

Thixendale

Ruin

Water Dale

Wolds Way BW

Ruin

BW

Birdsall

Burythorpe

PH

Farm

Roman Road

N

Route 13. **GRIMSTON BROW - WOLDS WAY -** **THIXENDALE**

Distance	16.5 miles: off road 9.25 miles; on road 7.25 miles.
Time	2 hours 30 mins to 3 hours .
Grade	3/3: Medium to Hard in places depending on conditions.
Terrain	Undulating brows and valleys, some woodland and open farm land.
Surface	Smooth tarmac roads, hard-packed lanes, single-track and rough, ill-defined field tracks.
Maps	OS Map Sheet 100 & 101 Landranger Series.

This route could prove difficult in places for the inexperienced rider, but would be worth trying with more experienced riders as companions, who could offer help if need be. Having said that, do not be put off. The hard sections are relatively short, and after a spell of dry weather, should not prove too difficult. The single track, if approached with caution, should again provide an enjoyable experience for the novice rider as well as the more seasoned veteran. The entire route is picturesque, with points of interest cropping up everywhere, for those who prefer a more leisurely approach to their riding. But at the same time, it is demanding enough in places, to give a buzz to the more athletic rider.

THE ROUTE:
From the start in North Grimston, GR 843677, go SE up the road to a quarry on the L. Shortly after the quarry, the road divides and you must go L. Continue along the B1253 until you meet a BW on the R. It is clearly marked and easy to see. Go down this loose stone track which descends quickly to a TJ. Enter this road carefully, watch out for fast-moving vehicles. Go L up to the village of Wharram le

Street. (Change to Map 101 which you will need for the next 2.5 mls.)

At the village continue SO at the XR along the B1248 past the sign, indicating the historic, ruin at Wharram Percy, and, after 1.5 miles, look out for a BW off to the R, across the road from a small wood (GR879639). Go R and follow the BW alongside a wall on the left. This grassy track continues for 0.5 mile, eventually emerging onto a tarmac lane at an offset XR. Here it joins the Wolds Way. Go SO through a metal gate (GR869635), following the BW signs. (Many of the tracks are Wolds Way or Centenary BW routes so watch out for walkers and hose riders. Please be polite and give way).

As you ride along this grassy ridge above Deep Dale, you pass a wooded area on the left. Soon after you come to the beginning of a second wood, directly across the valley from Wharram Percy Farm. Here on the L is a BW. Follow it into an open field and a wider track. Just ahead is an old red-brick ruin. This is Wolds House. Go past the house, keeping to the track as it bears L and begins to descend. Do not turn off this track, but look out for a BW sign on the L at a J. Turn R to a wooden gate alongside a hedge. Go through and follow the BW sign pointing to the L.

This next part of the route can be quite exciting as the ST descends, steadily at first as it dodges past bushes on either side, and then finishing with a fairly steep, bumpy ride down to a gate leading onto a road. Go R along the road to Thixendale, turning R into the village at a staggered crossroads.

At this point you may feel like a rest or perhaps something to eat. There is a pub, the Cross Keys, just off to the R if you need refreshment. If you wish to keep going, continue along the road up Water Dale valley. Just at the edge of the village, by a farm on the left, you will see a BW sign pointing to the L. Follow the track through a gate and into a field. **A word of warning here**, Do not take the more obvious track going off and up to the right. Go L along the grassy track following the valley bottom. Continue along, passing through a gate, then shortly after passing a curious earthworks, which cuts across the track, the route divides. Bear R to a gate and a BW sign. Go through the gate and follow the grassy track as it climbs steadily. This section is hard going, but fortunately short, as it emerges at a farm via a gate. Turn L onto a welcome tarmac lane and S0 to a TJ with an old Roman Road. Follow this road, with tumuli and burial grounds scattered on either side of it, for about 2 miles. Over the brow of a hill it runs into a TJ. Go across the road and through a gate. Follow the rough track down for a short distance and then turn R through another gate into a field. A BW sign points the way, as a series of single tracks spread out in front of you. So you take the high road and I'll take the low road and we'll both arrive at Mount Ferrant Farm at the same time! The choice of route through the field is not easy, but the higher route is probably the better one. A series of gates and a short muddy stretch, lead you into the farm. Follow the surfaced lane as it winds to the right and out of the farm and continue along this picturesque, tree-lined avenue to a TJ. Go R on the classified road as it heads towards the interesting little village of Birdsall. As you continue following the road, it passes the grounds of Birdsall House on the left, with a ruined church adjacent to the house. Soon afterwards, as the road skirts below another church to the left, it meets a private road. Keep on the main road bearing right. After 1/4 ml take the narrow lane which forks to the R down the short lane to a gate. Go through into a field and follow an indistinct track to the L, alongside a hedgerow.

Cross the fields and go through the gates until you come to a ruined red brick building. Go L through the gate just before the building - the BW sign points diagonally across to another metal gate on the other side of the field. **Do not go through it**. Keep R alongside the hedge and head for a small wood at the end of the field, where you will find a gateway. Another sign also appeared at this stage, warning travellers to be aware of a bull! The one I saw did not seem to be the slightest bit interested, despite my companions attempts at weaving his red-framed Mountain Bike all over the place

Go through a second gate and into another field, carry SO and exit via a metal gate which leads onto a road. Go across the road and follow the BW signs along a track to more BW signs at a wooden gate. Go through the gate and bear L up a grassy single track. Follow the ST as it winds R round a hill, before descending down a ST under a disused railway viaduct and onto the track leading over the stream, back to the start in North Grimston.

The bleak remains of Wold House on Cow Wold

A typical woodland track in the Wolds.

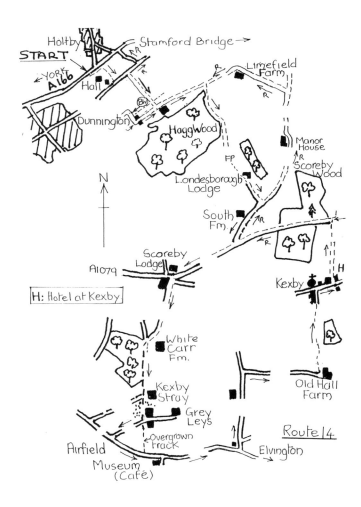

14

Holtby

Stamford Bridge →

START

← YORK A166

Hall

Limefield Farm

Dunnington

BW

Hagg Wood

Manor House

FP

Scoreby Wood

Londesborough Lodge

South Fm.

Scoreby Lodge

A1079

H: Hotel at Kexby

Kexby

H

White Carr Fm.

Kexby Stray

Grey Leys

Overgrown Track

Old Hall Farm

Route 14

Elvington

Airfield Museum (Café)

Route 14   DUNNINGTON - ELVINGTON.

Distance	13.5 miles: off-road 9.1 miles; on road 4.4 miles.
Time	1.5 to 2 hours.
Grade	2/2.
Terrain	Flat arable farm land, woodland.
Surface	Hard-pack, green lanes, roads.
Maps	OS Map Sheet 105 Landranger.

This route is ideal for the novice rider. It is mainly flat and uses BWs and surfaced lanes. Some short stretches of BW may be difficult after bad weather, but should not deter the enthusiast. Because main roads have to be used to link the off-road sections, care should be taken at these points. There are many places of interest around the route, some are worth taking time to visit. For example, the Aircraft Museum at Elvington, where you can also get a good cup of tea and a sticky bun at the café. Alternatively, you could make Elvington Village your half way break for refreshment at the local pub.

THE ROUTE:
Holtby Village is just off the A166 road between York and Stamford Bridge.

    From the village, go back to the junction with the A166. Watch out for fast traffic as you cross the road. Turn R towards York. After 100 yds, look out for the partially hidden wooden BW sign on the L — GR674586. The track goes through a narrow, wooden gate between some bushes and climbs L up a short single track. Follow this track as it skirts the fenced boundary of Dunnington Hall - the private golf course can be seen on your right as you head down to a TJ with a C road. Turn L and go down the road, looking out for a

BW sign on your R after 200 yds. Follow the fast track down to a recently built, red-brick house. Do not go SO — there is no official right of way, even though it may appear so. About 100 yds before the house (BW on map), turn R along a BW that crosses a field on an ST. Follow the ST until it emerges at a tarmac lane by Hagg Farm. Go L, then follow the lane as it bears L past Hagg Farm and takes you back on another bridleway running parallel to the lane you have just left. This leads you to the red-brick house that you could see earlier. Go SO in front of this house and follow the track until you come to a gate. Go through it, turn R and continue along the edge of Hagg Wood. Riding along this track in autumn can be likened to riding on marbles, there are so many marbles on the ground. Shortly after leaving Hagg Wood, the BW briefly changes status and becomes a FP (GR 690528). Physically it does not alter in width, **however one must dismount and walk the short distance to Londesborough Lodge Farm, and continue to walk through the farmyard.**

Go through the gate and the BW continues on the other side of the Lodge, soon turning R onto a tarmac track. It carries on to a TJ, where one turns R past South Farm on the right and shortly after arrive at a second TJ. Go R again and follow this tree-lined road to Scareby Lodge where you will meet the A1079 main road. Go straight across, again looking out for fast traffic on this busy route.

About 3/4 mile down this hard-pack track you will pass White Carr Farm on your L. Pass the farm, keeping to the BW running alongside the aptly named Rabbit Warren - a wooded area of oak, birch , ash and the inevitable rabbit. The surface of this track would be hard going after bad weather: fortunately it is only short and soon brings you to Kexby Stray, a small farm directly in front of you. The route appears to go right at this junction on a well-defined track; however, there is a wooden BW sign pointing S0 through an overgrown trail of burdock and nettles, between an avenue of trees. This short but rough section emerges at a TJ after about 100 yds onto a wide track., near Grey Leys Farm. Turn R at this junction and follow the track to the B 1228 road. Turn L and follow this road towards Elvington village.

You are now about halfway around the route and Elvington Airfield (used regularly for motor speed tests and drag racing) is on the right. There is a café here and the possibility of refreshment if you need it. There is also the museum if you have time to look round it. Take care as you cross the road if you intend stopping here,

Continue along the road to Elvington, looking out for a school on your L and shortly afterwards, turn L up the road signposted Kexby 2.5 miles. Follow the road for 3/4 mile, looking out for the sign on the R to Old Hall Farm. Cross the road and follow the track down to the farm. After passing a small house on the left and just before the farm, the track divides. Take the L track to a large metal gate which leads into a field. The route lies SO across the field on a grassy track. Keep going SO through a number of gates, the track gradually improving as it approaches a TJ with the main road (A1079) through Kexby village. Directly across the road from where you emerge is the sired church of Kexby. Cross the road and turn R. After 200 yds look out for a large hotel sign on the side of a building on your L. A partly hidden BW sign points L up a track alongside the hotel. Follow this track for 1/2 mile, and then turn L as the track goes alongside Scareby Wood. This pleasant, wooded section eventually opens out into a clearing after 1/2 mile and meets a surfaced road coming in from the R. In fact it is the road you came on earlier from Londesborough Lodge. Go R down this road and continue SO. Do not turn off left to Londesborough Lodge but carry on to Scoreby Manor House. The road is well surfaced as it passes the house and bears left. Continue along this road for 1/4 mile, then fork L as the road divides.

At Lime Field Farm, the road enters the farmyard. Take care here and stay on the rough track going R alongside a Dutch barn. The hard-pack track continues to a gate, which you came through earlier in the day. Go SO through the gate and continue to the red-brick house. From here you can retrace your route back to Holtby village and the start of the ride.

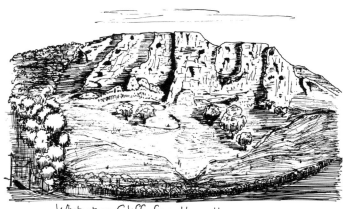

Whitestone Cliff from the valley

The bridleway route at the start of the Riveaulx route.

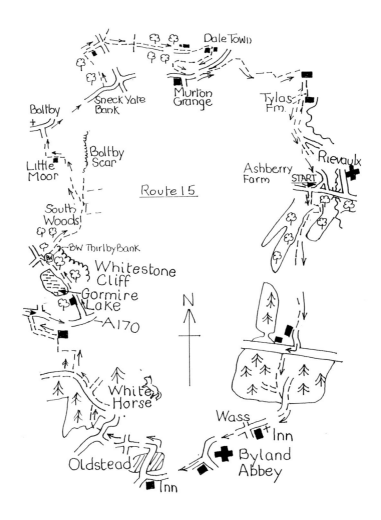

15

Dale Town

Sneck Yate Bank

Murton Grange

Tylas Fm.

Boltby

Little Moor

Boltby Scar

Ashberry Farm

START

Rievaulx

Route 15

South Woods

BW Thirlby Bank

Whitestone Cliff

Gormire Lake

A170

N

White Horse

Wass

Inn

Byland Abbey

Oldstead

Inn

Route 15   RIEVAULX - WHITESTONE CLIFF.

Distance	19.5 miles: off road 10.5; on road 9 miles.
Time	3 to 3 hours 30 mins
Grade	3/4
Terrain	Open farm land, moorland, woodland, hilly in places.
Surface	Tarmac lanes, bridleways, single track and grass tracks.
Maps	OS Map, Sheet 100 Landranger Series.

This is one of the most picturesque routes with a variety of scenic views and testing tracks. From the start, just along the road from Rievaulx Abbey, the scene is set for the ride. A tree-lined lane leads from the Abbey down to a small bridge near Ashberry Farm, nestling in this quiet little valley, but there is some hard riding before you return to this tranquil place. There are some technical sections and steep ascents as well as descents to contend with - not a route for the inexperienced or novice rider. Leave yourself plenty of time and make sure you take along a good OS map, preferably 1; 25000.

If you enjoy landscape photography, this is the route for your camera.

THE ROUTE.
From Ashberry Farm (GR 572845), go S over the bridge bearing R and following the road for 100 yds., then take the BW on your L and proceed up the rough track until it meets an even rougher track coming down from the R as the track you are on begins to level off and bear left. Go R up this track and notice the BW sign on your left almost hidden from view, pointing R uphill. This is a fairly steep and rough pathway, leading up between trees to a clearing. Just

ahead is a gate. Go SO through the gate and into a shallow gully lined with gorse bushes. Follow this gully as it heads up through fields, passing through two gates on the way. On entering the next flat open field, the gully and track are no longer visible. Go SO across this field; the ground is fairly flat but begins to rise again as the gully reappears.

On the right are two distinctive tumuli and just ahead is a large wooden barn . Go through the metal gate (there were two friendly sheep dogs in makeshift kennels here) and carry on to a second gate which leads you to a TJ with the A170 road. Turn R along this road, then almost immediately L onto a marked BW. This is a pleasant wooded trail, a bit rutted in places. Ignore a better looking track turning to the right, instead go SO through the woods, keeping to this track, bearing L at a clearing until you come to a TJ with a tarmac road at a gate. Go R and follow this steeply descending hill to the village of Wass.

At the XR, the Wombwell Arms has an Egon Ronay award menu, if you have time to spare! If not, go SO towards Byland Abbey. As you pass the ruins of the Abbey on your left, you cannot help but marvel at the skills of the Monks who built it centuries ago.

At this point, take the road to the R signposted to Kilburn and Oldstead, passing a second pub on the corner as you do so. For the next two miles you are following the tarmac lane. Continue on through Oldstead Village, bearing R as the road divides by another public house. The road carries SO at the next XR and then, after 1/2 mile, as the road comes to a junction, turn R towards the famous White Horse cliff, carved out of the chalk on the hill side. As the road begins to climb steeply, take the BW on the L. The track is wide at first, but then it changes to a ST as it climbs steadily through pine trees, eventually meeting a forestry track at an acute angle. Bear L along this forest track, which has a good surface, heading down through the pine woods to a J. Keep L here and go downhill again until the track begins to bend to the left. At this point, look out for a partially hidden BW sign on the right, indicating a ST down through a hedge. Follow this rough track down across a field to a farm. Continue to follow the BW signs which skirt the farm to the left. This part of the route has been reduced to a narrow strip which is difficult to ride on, but fortunately it does not last long. Go R through a gate, following the track as it crosses a narrow wooden bridge and then continues alongside a wire fence, meeting a sur-faced lane at a J. Go L along this lane which meets the main A170 road at the beginning of Sutton Bank.

This is a busy road, **take care as you cross it** and turn R up the hill. Continue riding past the first BW sign and carry on until the road begins to dip down again. Look out for the second BW sign on the left (There may well be a new sign post indicating Gormire Lake now). Go L and follow this road up a hill past some buildings on the left and continue to a gateway. Go through the gate and you will see Gormire Lake in front of you. Follow the ST through the wood, as it bears R and skirts round the lake. This is a very picturesque part of the route, but be aware of walkers who may also be using the same track.

Just before the track reaches a road, you have to turn R (see [BW] on map), almost back on yourself. (Look out for the signpost: BW Thirlby Bank). The track begins to climb in earnest; as it gets steeper, it is difficult to obtain any grip unless the weather has been very dry. (The going is difficult and presents quite a challenge — granny ring for some perhaps?) As you climb up through the Sweet Chestnut trees, the track opens out at the top onto the Cleveland Way. The view from here is breathtaking, overlooking, as it does, the plains below.

Take the track which heads off left along the top of the cliffs, overlooking South Woods below on the left side. Continue along this grassy ST for a few hundred yards to a wooden signpost indicating Boltby. Bear L down this ST to a gate, go through and SO. This track could be muddy in wet weather; it is also steep and rutted in places. Eventually it reaches a TJ with a hard-pack forest road. Go across and follow the BW sign and continue to a TJ. Turn R following the BW sign to Boltby. As this track descend it passes through more gates before reaching an open field for a final, fast descent to a gate. Go through and follow the well made track which leads across a ford to a surfaced road heading to Boltby. At Boltby Village, turn R at the TJ and continue up the road for 1.5 miles to Sneck Yate Bank. This is a short but steep tarmac-surfaced climb. Look out for the Cleveland Way BW sign on the left on a sharp bend. Turn L and follow the track through the wood which continues to a gate. Go through and SO on a rising grassy track to a second gate at a J with a forest road. Turn R and follow the tarmac road to a farm. (**At the farm, please dismount and walk through**.)

Continue along the hard-pack track to a staggered XR. Go across the track to a gate and turn R to follow the track alongside a wall to a crossing track. Carry SO, go through a gate and continue down to the next gate. Go SO on a broad hard-pack track to a gap in a dry-stone wall, where bear R through the gap and head towards a gate. Go through the gate and straight ahead, dropping down a steep rocky track which eventually emerges onto a forestry road. Turn R on this road and look for the BW sign on the right. Turn L dropping across a field to a clump of trees. Go around the left-hand side of the trees and drop to a stream crossing just before some derelict buildings. The track continues past these buildings and rises gently to Dale Town Farm. Bear R through the farm, and at the gate follow the BW sign to your right. Keep to the left of the large trees and follow a rather indistinct track up the hill to an information board.

At the board turn R along a ST which leads to a hardpack forest road. Turn L and follow the road up to a metal gate. At the top where it meets a road just before the Murton Grange junction, turn L and continue along the road for about 200 yards. Just as the road begins to descend, look out for a BW sign on the left which directs you onto a rough track, on the right, running parallel to the road. Go through the barrier and follow the track as it bears R and changes to a grassy track. The surrounding area is a pine plantation (Cliff Wood).

Follow the route as it gradually descends through the woods for over a mile. As you come onto a rough, surfaced track, it bears left. Don't follow it. Instead, take the less defined track up to the R and follow the BW signs through a gate and into a field. Skirt round this field to the L, close to the edge. The track is indistinct at this point, until it reappears just as you start to descend to Barnclose Farm. Go through the wooden gate into the farm yard. It may be a good procedure to walk this short bit round to the R because of the close proximity to the farm. Once through the farm, follow the tarmac-surfaced lane to the next farm, Tylas Farm, which is up a slight incline. Go through the wooden gate and turn R up a short climb and over a cattle grid.

The remainder of the route is on this surfaced lane. As it dips and climbs, it is possible to see Rievaulx Abbey down the valley to the left. This is Rye Dale. At a J, go L, following the road to a fork. Go R down the steep hill to Ashberry Farm and the start point.

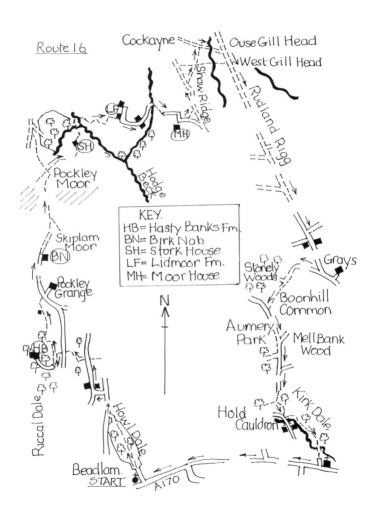

16

Route 16

Cockayne — Ouse Gill Head — West Gill Head

Shaw Ridge

Rudland Rigg

LF

MH

SH

Pockley Moor

Hodge Beck

KEY.
HB= Hasty Banks Fm.
BN= Birk Nob
SH= Stork House
LF= Lidmoor Fm.
MH= Moor House

Skiplam Moor

BN

Pockley Grange

HB

Riccal Dale

Howl Dale

Beadlam. START

A170

N

Stonely Woods

Grays

Boonhill Common

Aumery Park

Mell Bank Wood

Kirk Dale

Hold Cauldron

Route 16   BEADLAM - POCKLEY MOOR - RUDLAND RIGG

Distance	21 miles; off road 15 miles; on road 6 miles.
Time	3 hours 30 mins to 4 hours 30 mins.
Grade	3/3
Terrain	Undulating, varying from woodland in the valleys to open moor with exposed areas on higher ground.
Surface	Smooth tarmac lanes, single grassy tracks, hard-pack bridleways, mostly rideable.
Maps	OS Map Sheet 100 Landranger Series.

This route is again, typical of the lower Yorkshire Moors area with isolated hamlets linked by well-worn bridle tracks crossing the moorland. The scenery is varied, with the softer woodland areas in the valleys contrasting with the harsh wildness of the moors. It is not a difficult route, but there are a number of alternative tracks which may be taken, depending on the conditions at the time of riding. These occur mainly in the Bransdale area near the village of Cockayne: a brief explanation of the alternative routes will be given.

THE ROUTE.
Starting from the lane next to the wooden - spired church, GR 655847, follow the track through the woods until it emerges at a junction with a tarmac lane. Continue up Howl Lane, and follow it as it bends sharply left then right when it becomes Beadlam Rigg. Shortly after passing Low Farm, look out for the BW on the L. Go through the gate, cross the field and enter the wood. The track swings to the right and climbs for a short distance before crossing a field to a gate. Go through the gate and cross the road to a gate leading into a field with a sign for Hasty Banks Farm. The track

goes across the field to the L; follow it for a short distance to a wire fence on the right. Go sharp R alongside this fence, keeping to the top side of the woods on the left . This track is grassy and not always obvious, but follow it through to a clearing and into a field at the top of a bank. Looking straight ahead, you will see what appears to be several tracks going in different directions. Go down the banking and keep SO as the track climbs past a small red-brick animal shelter. At this point there is little sign of a track, but continue SO up the field to a gateway which leads onto the road opposite the entrance to Pockley Grange. Go L along the road for 1 mile, to Birk Nab.

At this point you leave the road and follow the rough track beyond the gate ahead of you. This is the lower end of Hagg Common. After a mile of steady climbing on the heather-flanked track, you come to a junction with a wide ochre-coloured track, deeply rutted in places but easy to ride: this is Pockley Moor. Continue NW along this track for 3/4 mile to a cross tracks. This section is not too obvious, but take the track to the R and follow it down to the ruin called Stork House. Again the heather often obscures the route as you scan ahead, so be alert.

At the ruins, go through the courtyard to the left, exit by a small wooden gate and head down a grassy pathway to a signpost indicating the direction to Lidmoor. Turn R and go down the steep slope to a stream in the picturesque valley bottom. The ford crossing looks too deep for bikes to cross, so use the narrow footbridge.

After crossing the stream, follow the track to the R as it climbs up to Lidmoor Farm. Go through the gates and pass the farm on the lower side, joining a hard-pack track on the R after climbing up a short slope. Follow this track as it skirts round more farm houses and soon after leaving Moor House Farm, you can see a road at a TJ just ahead. Don't go SO, but turn onto a track to the L which cuts off the corner and takes you across to a TJ with the road going up Shaw Rigg. Go L and follow this road almost into Cockayne. Just after Cow Syke Farm, go through the gate by the stile on the R, which leads you onto a steep path climbing alongside a wall in the field. The path exits onto the moor via a gate and continues to follow the wood upward below a steep incline. The track bears right and continues to climb to the top of the moor. Stay on the right-hand track where it divides and you reach the Rudland Rigg track known as Westside Road. Turn R and follow this hard-packed track, which must have been a metalled surface at one time, as it climbs gently to the trig point before starting a long descent.

As stated earlier, there are alternative routes which can be taken from the point where you reach Cow Syke Farm. The first alternative is to take the route to the right by the farm which heads back simply up to Ouse Gill Head and joins the Rudland Rigg track near West Gill Head, to continue R along Westside Road.

The second alternative, is to take the BW on the R about 1/4 mile before the Spout House TJ. This rough track climbs less steeply than the others, but in summer it can be obscured in places, by heather. It joins the route coming up from Cow Syke Form, which should then be followed up to Ouse Gill Head and then on to Westside Road on Rudland Rigg.

Returning to the descent down Rudland Rigg, the track gradually changes to a tarmac surface. Ignore the first turn to the right and continue for almost a mile to a TJ on the right, opposite a place called Grays. Turn R and follow this narrow tarmac road as it bears left below an imposing hill. Where the road enters Stonely Woods, follow the track to the L by a sign. At the gate, go SO and cross the field, bearing right towards more woodland. Stay in the field and continue along the edge of the wood - there is no obvious track at this point, so head for the gate just ahead. Go through the gate and turn L onto a tarmac road. This road takes you along Sleightholme Dale and through the scenic Aurnery Park. Continue along the road for about 1 1/4 mile and at the top of a rise, you will see a wooden signpost to Hold Cauldron. The road bears sharp L, but continue along the trail to the R into Mell Bank Wood. Follow this track through the wood, ignoring any minor tracks leading off to left or right, go through a gate, and carry on down to Hold Cauldron Bridge. Just before the bridge, turn L through a gate and into a wood. The track is to the L and climbs quite steeply at first before levelling off as it continues through Kirk Dale Valley along a narrow woodland track.

Take care along this section of track - it's winding and the tree roots can be slippery in places where they cross the track. The track has been running alongside Hodge Beck which (at the time of riding the route) appeared to have diverted course just before the wooden bridge, leaving a dry river bed where the bridge crossed. Follow the track over the bridge and continue on past the church on the left up to a TJ with a road. Turn R and follow the road as it joins the AI70 just before Nawton Village. Carry on the main road through Nawton and back to the start point in Beadlam.

Overlooking Dale Town towards Hawnby Moors

The track through Mell Bank Wood

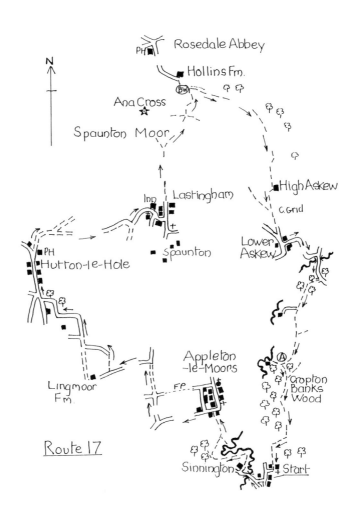

17

Rosedale Abbey

PH

Hollins Fm.

BW

Ana Cross

Spaunton Moor

High Askew

C. Grid

Inn   Lastingham

Lower Askew

Spaunton

PH
Hutton-le-Hole

Appleton -le-Moors

Cropton Banks Wood

FP.

Lingmoor Fm.

Route 17

Sinnington   Start

Route 17.   SINNINGTON - SPAUNTON MOOR - ROSEDALE ABBEY.

Distance	19.5 miles; off road 16 miles; on road 3.5 miles.
Time	2.5 to 3 hours.
Grade	3/3 Could be hard going in places, depending on conditions.
Terrain	Some sheltered woodland, open fields, moorland stretches which can be exposed in places.
Surface	Tarmac lanes, hard-pack bridleways, single-track (muddy in wet weather).
Maps	OS Sheet 100 Landranger Series.

If 1 was asked to pick out a selection of my favourite off-road routes, this one would certainly be near the top. It is mostly off road and rideable, taking in some excellent scenery, with some good climbs and descents. The villages of Sinnington, Lastingham, Rosedale Abbey and others in the area, are all picturesque and contain welcoming hostelries with atmosphere and old world charm. I can vouch for the welcome, having descended on a local pub — the Blacksmith's Arms at Lastingham — one wet and sleeting day in May. My friends and I were made most welcome and we were allowed to dry our wet clothing by the open fire, whilst we ate an excellent lunch.

THE ROUTE.
From the village green in Sinnington (GR745857), head W over the bridge and turn R on the BW immediately after the bridge. The BW runs alongside some cottages on the left and the river on the right. The BW continues to follow the river bank and soon you enter a wood through a wooden gate. Here the track becomes rough and just before a climb, go through a second gate into a wooded area.

This too could be muddy in places, and care should be taken negotiating the roots. A third gate leads you out into an open field. Cross
the field to a gate. Go through and over a wooden bridge to the L.
The track now climbs steadily to the village of Appleton-le-Moors.
As you go through a gate by farm buildings, turn L on the tarmac
lane. Go SO for 0.75 miles and look out for a BW on the R near a
left bend in the road. Go R and follow the dirt path across fields.
Continue SO at a path crossing; then after a further half mile, turn L
and follow the track which descends through a wood to a gateway
which exits onto a road. Turn R along the road into Hutton-le-Hole.
This is an attractive village and very popular with tourists, who seem
to flock here by the bus-load.

Go through the village, turning R by the pub, climb the hill by the
carpark and follow the road to Lastingham. This is a pleasant little
village and the Blacksmith's Arms makes a good stopping point if
you wish to have a rest. From the pub, go past the church on the
right and then take a L turn at the TJ, then, as the road dips, turn L
up a street between rows of houses, which eventually leads you to
the gateway onto Spaunton Moor BW.

The BW is quite wide and in dry weather, the hard-pack track
makes riding easy. In wet conditions the climbing becomes more
difficult, as rivulets of water find their way down the track, carving
deeper channels each year. Follow the track due N for about 1.25
miles, ignoring any tracks to left or right, then bear R to the NE for
0.75 mile to a track which crosses the one you are on. This track
comes down from Ana Cross, which can be seen on the horizon to
the left. Continue SO at this XR — the route is now ST and it winds
its way between the heather bushes to a short but steep drop. The
track bears R then L leading you down to a farm building (Hollins
Farm).

If you wish, you can follow this track as it widens out, and heads
towards Rosedale Abbey, where you will find a pub and café for

refreshments. If you don't choose to go to the pub or café, but wish to continue on the route, you will have to turn R at BW (GR 734943) onto the ST running alongside a wall, just above Hollins Farm. (If you have descended past a wooden BW sign on your way down to Hollins Farm, you have gone too far past this turning by the wall).

   You are now on the return route. This ST rolls and winds its way across the lower side of the Moor, interrupted in places by streams, which cut across the track creating interesting diversions. Eventually after much winding about, the track reaches High Askew Farm. Turn R up the hard-surfaced road by the farm gate and follow this road until it descends quickly to a TJ. Continue SO (bearing L) down to Lower Askew Village. As you enter the village, turn L between the farm houses, following the road to a TJ near a bridge. Go R over the bridge. Climb the hill for a short distance and just as the road starts to bear left, a BW track can be seen on the R by a wooden bench. This track can be muddy when the weather is bad, but fortunately it does not spoil the ride because it does not last long. As the track emerges into a clearing, it divides. Take the L track up to a wooden gate. Go through, following the narrow track as it enters Cropton Banks Wood. The trail is crossed by tree roots, so care should be taken. As the track descends, look out for a track coming in from the left — see 'A' on the map. Go L up this track, climbing to the top of the woods to a trail which follows the edge of the wood. Again take care, the tree roots can catch you out in places. Continue to follow the track to a gateway leading onto a narrow path between hedges which eventually turns R onto a wider track then L as it enters the old Sinnington Hall grounds. If you look back near the church, you can see the remnants of some previous, ancient, arched windows, now incorporated into a barn-like building. Take a R turn as you pass the church on the corner. This takes you back to the start point on the village green at Sinnington.

The track through Cropton Banks Wood.

The long and winding road over Spaunton Moor.

Group on the track following the River Seven near Fuelscot Wood.

18

Rosedale
Abbey
Hollins
Farm
Ana
Cross
HR
Moor Route
HR
HR
CG
High Askew
Low
Wind
Hill
Head
House
Lower
Askew
Cropton
Inn
R
R
R
R
R
CROPTON
FOREST
Lodge
Return
Route
R
R
R
R
Cropton
Banks
wood
Cawthorne
N
HR = High Route
CG = Cattle Grid
= Return Route
START
Sinnington
A 170
Route 18.

Route 18   **SINNINGTON - ROSEDALE ABBEY -**
                      CROPTON FOREST.

Distance	24 miles; off-road 20 miles; on road 4 miles
Time	4 to 5 hours
Grade	3/3. More demanding in wet weather.
Terrain	Undulating, moorland and forest, long fast descents.
Surface	Tarmac road, stone-surfaced tracks, single moorland tracks, forest tracks
Maps	OS Map Sheet 100 Landranger Series.

Only a short distance away from the lower-lying areas around York, you will find the foothills of the North York Moors and the beginnings of the large forestry estates. Pickering is just on the lower edge and provides the gateway to the wealth of off-road tracks to the north. Five miles west of Pickering, just off the A170, is the picturesque village of Sinnington, GR 745857. The route starts here and provides you with an entertaining variety of off-road riding, probably more suitable for riders with some experience. However the route may be lengthened or shortened as you wish, since there are many alternative opportunities.

THE ROUTE
There are a number of parking places in Sinnington. Most mountain bikers and walkers seem to opt for the road beside the village green, although consideration must be given to the residents as too many parked vehicles may cause offence.
From the green, follow the road along the right side of the small chapel to a post barrier in the road. Go through and immediately turn R up a hill to a second church. Follow the road as it bears L in

front of the church. You will see a BW sign pointing the way onto a track. Follow this track up through the fields, alongside the hedgerow and eventually into a wood. The track now becomes a ST as it climbs up through the wood. After 1/3 mile the path divides. Take the L path dropping down towards the river. Ignore the first turn off to the R but soon after, (about 0. 1 mile) turn R and continue along a path which appears to be taking you back up the hill, but levels off and passes through a number of gates until the track splits three ways. Go SO through more gates until you emerge onto a road. Follow the road down and turn L over a bridge, signposted Lastingham. As the road meanders through Lower Askew, turn R at a TJ and soon after as the road bears L, continue SO up a narrower lane which soon becomes a waymarked BW. The surface becomes rougher as the track climbs to a cattle grid.

From this point you have a choice of routes, either L, up over Spaunton Moor (see 'HR' on map) — *see notes for this route further on in text — or continue SO along a lower, more sheltered route. If you choose to carry SO from the cattle grid, follow the track as it drops down to a farm, High Askew. Just before the farm gate, turn L onto a badly marked, grassy track, which runs alongside the farm boundary. This section can be wet in places as the track crosses and re-crosses a water table. This an undulating single track, and as it climbs higher and becomes drier, you can look across the valley to the right and see Cropton Forest and the River Seven.

As the track begins to descend, you pass the steep track coming down from the left which is where the Spaunton Moor trail emerges, had you turned off earlier on the alternative route. You are now just a short distance from Hollins Farm and another decision - either, make the 3/4 mile journey SO to the pub just above Rosedale Abbey, for refreshments, or if you wish to continue, take the BW route off to the R and through a narrow gate shortly after the farm.

Both high and low routes continue from this point.

There is no obvious path through this field, but fortunately it is downhill. Keep close to the wall and head for the river crossing, either by ford or footbridge. Take care if you contemplate the ford crossing, it can be deep in places and slippery!

Continue, climbing up through rough pasture, keeping close to the hedge on the left as you head for Yatts Farm. Go through the gate to the left of the farm and onto the road. Turn R and look out for the BW sign almost immediately on your left, pointing the way up through another field via a gateway. At the top of this short climb, you enter a wood by a small gate. Again the track climbs steeply as it bears R through the wood to a gate which exits into a field just below a cottage. Follow the track as it crosses in front of the cottage, through a gateway, and turns R onto a more clearly defined track back into the wood again. At this point there are three different tracks. Take the track SO which leads up a gentle slope to a road which crosses it at the top. Turn L and follow the road for 1 mile to a BW sign on the right, just before a wooded area. This track can be wet in places, but follow the waymarks and be particularly careful to look out for where the track dives back into the wood between an avenue of trees, emerging soon after into an open field, whose track leads down to a TJ with a road. Turn L along the road and then immediately R downhill to Low Wind Hill, a small farmstead at the stream crossing. There is a footbridge back to the left if you don't fancy the ford. Either way, once across the stream, follow the track, not clearly marked, up the hillside to Cropton Forest. This is probably the most confusing bit of track to follow - going up the hill there appears to be signpost indicating a footpath, whereas coming down, the signs show it to be a BW! The reason for this ambiguity is not at all clear, but a BW does exist over to the left. Unfortunately, it too is not very well defined. If you are in doubt as to which track you are on, walk the relatively short distance up the field to the gate at the top and go through onto the forest track and turn R.

This bumpy track follows the edge of the forest for about 0.75 mile and then reaches a gate which takes you onto the Forestry Commission tracks. The going is much easier from now on with the exception of a couple of stretches which can be difficult if the weather has been wet. Carry on along the track until another track comes up from the right. Ignore this track and go SO up the one you are on. Soon you will come to a left bend and a BW sign pointing SO up a grassy track between an avenue of pines. This section of track requires full concentration - fallen trees and boggy hollows are there to trap the unwary, but it's great fun to ride. The track emerges onto the forest trail which drops tantalizingly down a straight trail to the right. Hard luck! Go SO and continue along the BW, which is again rough and difficult to ride but soon emerges onto one of those fast, downhill forest tracks. This one is the well-known Sutherland Road, which is the only official BW route through Cropton Forest — **please stay on it**. Follow this track past Skelton Banks Farm and up a tarmac-surfaced climb to a TJ. Go R here along High Lane, for 1 mile to the village of Cropton.

Continue L through the village, past the old chestnut tree on the triangular green and follow the road past the pub on the right. Immediately after the pub turn R along the BW and follow this narrow track until you reach a three-way junction. Ignore the routes to the left and right, and go SO through the gate and into a field. Cross this field as it climbs slightly to the right and takes you back into Cropton Banks Wood which you were in earlier in the day. This is a ST and continues along the top edge of the wood to the point where you turned off down into the wood on your outward journey. Turn L down this track, only this time go straight down to a gate just before a cottage and the river. Turn L and follow the gnarly, root-infested track as it winds its way along the lower edge of the wood. Just over 1/3 mile along this track, turn L and climb up through the wood to the track at the top. Turn R and you can follow this track the short distance back into Sinnington Village and the start.

*The high route (see [HR] on map). If you decide to go L at the cattle grid and head over Spaunton Moor, the track is quite wide and easily followed as it climbs northwards for the next 2 miles towards Ana Cross. About 1/2 mile from the cross, just visible as a trig point on the sky line, the main track is crossed by a minor track. Turn R and follow this track for 1/4 mile to where the track seems to become a narrow path cut into the heather. Do not continue following this path, but bear R across an open stretch of moorland, still heading down, until the trail becomes more obvious as it bears L again and continues to descend steeply to the BW coming in from the R on the lower trail route. Just ahead is Hollins Farm and, shortly after, the small gateway into the field.

The Blacksmith's Arms
Lastingham

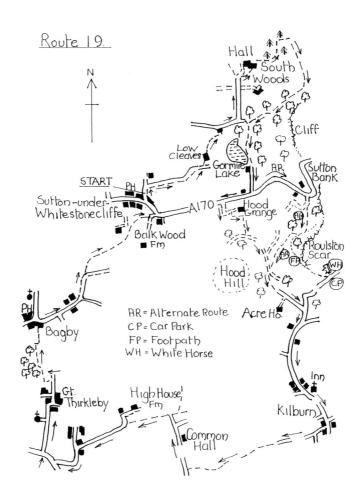

19

Route 19.

N

Hall
South Woods
Cliff
Low Cleaves
Gormire Lake
Sutton Bank
START
PH
AR
Sutton-under-Whitestonecliffe
A170
Hood Grange
Balk Wood Fm
Roulston Scar
AR
FP
WH
CP
Hood Hill
PH
Bagby
AR = Alternate Route
CP = Car Park
FP = Footpath
WH = White Horse
Acre Ho.
Inn
Gt. Thirkleby
High House Fm
Kilburn
Common Hall

ROUTE 19. THE WHITE HORSE LOOP.

Distance:	14 miles; off road 11 miles; on road 3 miles.
Time:	2 hours 30 minutes.
Grade:	3/4.
Terrain:	Steep climbs, mixed woodland, open farm land, un dulating.
Surface:	Hard-packed tracks, single-track, tarmac lanes and woodland earth tracks.
Maps:	OS Map Malton & Pickering. Sheet 100 Landranger Series.

This is an exciting ride, to the west of Ryedale, featuring Sutton Bank with its panoramic views and attendant steep climbs and descents through woodland. It is followed by gentle undulating tracks through scenic farm lands in the Kilburn area. This is not a ride for the novice, even though the distance is relatively short, but it is extremely rewarding.

THE ROUTE.
From Sutton-Under-Whitestonecliffe, follow the A170 eastwards to where the road begins to bear R. Look out for the BW on the left at GR 487825 pointing down a lane between some cottages. Follow the bridle track for a short distance before turning R by a sign to Low Cleaves Caravan Park. Go through the farmyard to a metal gate. Continue through the gate bearing R onto a track below a wood. On entering a second field, the track becomes bumpy and when it reaches two metal gates you will see Whitestone cliffs straight ahead. Go through the red gate on the left and follow the track up past a house on your left until you arrive at a wooden gate. Go through the gate and turn R onto the road. Follow this for

0.25 mile to some cottages and take the track to the L, through a wooden gate, which leads on to a BW. Follow the bridleway to a second gate called Midgeholme Gate. Go SO following the bridleway sign. Ignore the next bridleway sign to Tang on the left, and bear R on the track leading to the house (Southwoods Hall). Before the house the track divides — keep R and follow this track to a gate into a farmyard. Turn R through the yard and go through a second gate into a field. Keep close to a wall on the left and make for a BW sign on a post. This is a steep grassy climb up through fields. It is well marked with BW signs on posts. On reaching a gate, go through into South Woods and follow the muddy track climbing all the time. Keep to the well-worn track as it bears sharp L at a J with a less used track. Again, climb to gate in a stone wall, and go through bearing R at the top and follow the cliff bridleway. This is a narrow ST and follows the cliff edge for just over a mile. Near a BW marker post, look out for where the track turns R and begins to descend down a gully into the woods. (If you miss this turning you will end up on the footpath which incidentally is much wider and better maintained than the bridleway).

The track descends quite steeply through the woods and eventually meets a TJ with another BW at the bottom of the valley. Turn L here and follow this interesting, winding, ST to Gormire Lake. The track ends at a gate just after the lake. Go through the gate and head down the wider roadway past a house on the right. Stop at the TJ with the main road (A170).

At this point there is a choice of return routes. If you would like to visit the famous White Horse of Kilburn, which was cut into the Corallian limestone in 1857 by a schoolmaster, called Hodgson, with the help of some school boys, and on the initiative of Thomas Taylor then follow the *alternative route* (See reference on map AR). The alternative route is described at the end of the main route.

MAIN ROUTE

Returning by the main route, having crossed the main road which is extremely busy at all times, turn R and ride up the short climb Then after about 0.5 mile, as you are descending, look out for the BW sign on your left which indicates a track to Hood Grange Farm. Go L and follow the track almost to the farm, but look for the BW signs on the right indicating the route through a gate into a field. Go R down the field and over the small wooden bridge to another gate. Turn L and follow the edge of this field as it skirts around the farm and eventually turns R up a ST which crosses a field leading to a wood. Hood Hill is directly ahead of you (but you do not have to climb it !). A short, root-strewn track up through this wood leads to a TJ onto a hard-pack forest trail. Turn L and climb steadily for a short distance to where the trail divides. Keep to the right and continue to where it begins to level off and then descends slightly. Be careful at this point (GR 508814), because it is all too easy to miss the BW turning on the right as there is no sign — soon to be remedied.) It is also at this point that the alternative route rejoins the main route.

Having found this track, turn R and follow its course parallel to the forest track for a short distance before descending into the woods. Continue following the ST which is quite difficult in places because of the off-camber and tree roots. There is also an added problem of short muddy stretches before you finally meet a wider, drier track which emerges at a TJ with a road which comes down from the White Horse carving. Turn R down the hill to a J and bear R on the road to Kilburn village. At Kilburn village there are a number of shops and an inn, where you can stop for refreshment. To continue, follow the road S through the village past the church on the left and continue for a short distance until you see the BW sign on the right. Turn R on the tarmac lane between the houses. Go SO until the track deteriorates as you go through an avenue of trees. The track opens out onto fields and follows the hedgerow round to a TJ with a tarmac lane. Turn R and follow the BW signs to a second TJ passing Common Hall on the right. Turn L at the TJ onto a hard-pack track leading to High House Farm. Just before the farm entrance turn L, following the BW signs along a grassy verge, turning R at the end of the fence. Follow the grass verge once more along the front of the farm fence eventually joining a tarmac lane which leads to Little Thirkleby. At the TJ turn L. At **all** the next three TJs, turn R — these are all on tarmac. This brings you to Great Thirkleby.

Go past the spired church in the field and follow the road around the bend to the right taking the first turn L. Go down hill turning L at the BW sign, which is on the right before a signpost saying sharp bend. Follow the grassy track across the field towards the wood, keeping the woods on the left, and skirt the field to a gate. Go through, passing the caravan park on the left and continue SO. At a TJ in the track go R for 20 yards then go L through the metal gate. Continue SO to a TJ with a road in Bagby village. Turn R go downhill for 3/4 of a mile to where the road bears right and look out for the metal gate on the left with a waymark arrow. Go through the gate onto the grassy track. Soon the route become less obvious, as the hedge you have been following on your left goes left, you must continue SO keeping to the left of the line of trees in the field, until you reach a hedge on the opposite side of the field. Turn R along the edge of the field to a metal gate on the left. Follow the waymark sign through the gate and bear L across the field to another gate. Go through and skirt the field to the R to yet another gate in the corner of the field. Go through and follow the hedgerow to a final gate which leads to a white limestone track. Turn L and follow the track to a TJ with a main road (A170). Turn L on the main road back to your starting point in Sutton-Under-Whitestonecliffe.

ALTERNATIVE ROUTE.
From the TJ with the A170 on the Sutton Bank road, turn L. The descent is short lived as you are soon confronted with the beginning of the infamous Sutton Bank climb. Fortunately you do not have to climb up the whole way. At the first hairpin bend, there is a track which leads off to the right — a Police sign, requesting NO PARKING is at the entrance. It is probably easier and safer to cross the road below this point and walk up to the track. **Be extra careful crossing this road; it is extremely busy**. Follow the track into the woods for a short distance to where the first sharp bend occurs. As the main track bears right do not follow it. Instead, follow the track that goes SO at the bend and heads off on a flat and fairly wide grassy track. The route continues just under an impressive cliff face on the left and the track surface gradually changes to hard-pack just before the bend at Roulston Scar (GR 513818) — easily recognised as it is a mass of creamy-coloured, Corallian limestone cliff). You will have to dismount at this point because the track now becomes a footpath. (You should have just gone past a track coming down from the left.) The BW that you need to take veers off down a totally obscure track and descends steeply through the woods on the right. (At the time of writing, I was informed by Helmsley National Parks Officers that this section of BW was due for extensive clearance work and improvement.)

If you want to view the White Horse of Kilburn the only access is along the hard-pack footpath SO PLEASE WALK THIS SHORT DISTANCE FOLLOWING THE WHITE ARROWS ON RED-CAPPED POSTS. The footpath will bring you to a large open carpark and a viewing area. If you do not wish to return to the main bridleway via this footpath go through the carpark and turn R down the tarmac road which leads to Kilburn village after 1.75 mls. Here you can pick up the main route again. If you do not visit the White Horse or have returned to Roulston Scar, then again look carefully for the bridleway that drops steeply into the woods in a westerly direction.

The next half mile of densely wooded track is difficult to follow and is equally difficult to describe. By heading due W from the main BW just below Roulston Scar, descend through the pine trees. This first part is very steep and technical so take care, use your discretion. After about 200 yards, bear L in a SW direction where the going is less steep as it follows the contours around. It is possible at this point to see below the main forest track which you are aiming for. Continue descending with care until you eventually emerge onto this forest track. At this point, GR508814, you will meet the main route (see note for main route).

The Spired Church Thirkleby

Crossing Stony Moor.

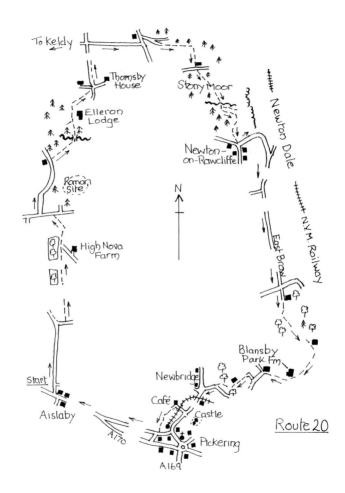

20

To Keldy

Thornsby House

Elleron Lodge

Roman Site

High Nova Farm

Start

Aislaby

A170

Stony Moor

Newton Dale

Newton-on-Rawcliffe

N

East Brow

N.Y.M. Railway

Blansby Park Fm

Newbridge

Café

Castle

Pickering

A169

Route 20

Route 20. STONY MOOR - NEWTON DALE - BLANSBY PARK.

Distance	16.5 mile; off road 11 miles; on road 5.5 miles
Time	2.5 to 3 hours
Grade	3/3
Terrain	open countryside, woodland, moorland, some forestry land.
Surface	Bridleways, hard-pack tracks, grassy tracks, tarmac lanes.
Maps	OS Map Sheet 100 Landranger Series.

This is an excellent route with such varied terrain, that there is bound to be something to suit most off-road riders. It provides alternative routes at one point, which can be selected according to individual needs. The route also provides a panoramic view of Newton Dale and the North York Moors Railway, along which, steam engines make their nostalgic journey, up and down the valley.

THE ROUTE.
From the start point, just after Aislaby village, GR 774857, head N up the lane alongside a wall with the village name on it. The tarmac surface gradually deteriorates after 0.75 mile as you progress towards the first turning at a junction. Turn R along a rough track and after a short distance, take the track to the L and head N again. Continue along this track for 1.75 mile, until it reaches a TJ with a road. Go L along the road to the first turn off on the R. Head down this road, passing a site of historic interest, (Roman), up to the R.

As you approach a building on the left, near the bottom of the hill, look out for the LINK sign on the right, just before the wood. Go R along this narrow track alongside the fir trees. Follow it as it descends and enters the wood. The track leads to a narrow wooden bridge over a stream. Bear L over the bridge, (or ford the river if it is shallow) and continue to follow the track as it goes through the pine trees on an obvious route to a clearing. Just to the left is Elleron Lodge partly concealed by woodland. Ahead, where the track meets a gate, a sign indicates a footpath to the left, but ignore that and go through the gate into a field. The track is indistinct, but heads diagonally across the field to a wooden gate, which opens onto a track to the right of a cottage. Go through the gate and turn R. Then at a junction with three more tracks, take the one to the L which does not have a tarmac surface. (At this point, if you look back, you will see the white waymark arrow on a blue topped post, pointing back to where you came from.) Continue up this hard-pack track for about 0.5 mile until you reach a XR.

The marker post points to Keldy Castle along the left route, but turn R and go along the straight track to a TJ with a road. Turn L up the road, then after a short distance of about 200 yds, turn R along a short track which divides at a red ROAD CLOSED sign. At this point, turn R through an open gate and follow the track alongside the wood on your left. Stay on this track as it passes through two gates. About 100 yds after going through the last gate, the ST turns R, following the waymark sign along a narrow track to a cottage on the left. Go through the gate by the cottage and you come out onto a crossing track. Go SO across this track, following the ST as it winds its way through trees across Stony Moor, aptly named because of the large rocks which traverse the pathway, making the route fairly technical, but entertaining. As the path dips down to a stream, it becomes steeper just before the point where you cross. Ford this shallow stream and go through the wooden gate on the L. The pathway widens at this point and could become muddy, depending on weather conditions. If it is dry, it is possible to climb this track all the way to the top, but adhesion is limited once the track becomes wet. An attempt to stop erosion, by laying logs across the track at intervals, helps the horse riders considerably, but does nothing to help climbing on a mountain bike in the wet!

At the top of this steep climb, the track emerges in Newton-on-Rawcliffe. Turn L down the lane between the avenue of trees and bushes. As you bear right, you are suddenly presented with, what is known locally as, 'the surprise view'. Indeed it is, because you look down into the narrow valley of Newton Dale, and the rail crossing at the quaint little station of Levisham, one of several stops along the North York Moors Railway.

After taking in this scene, continue along the widening track called East Brow. The surface is hard-pack and fast, before it meets a TJ with a road. Cross the road and follow the BW which continues straight up from East Brow passing through a gate and up to a farm on the left. Continue following this track, as it climbs towards a wood and passes through to High Blansby Farm. The track begins to level off as it crosses fields, skirting some more farm buildings as it continues over the fields. The track gets wider and easier to follow as it descends to West Farm. Just after the farm, the track divides near a wooded area. Take a sharp turn R to a gate with a waymark on it. Go through the gate and follow the track past an old farm building before entering a wood. The route through the wood is quite narrow, and can be a little rough in places. It eventually winds its way down to a gate which leads onto a tarmac lane. Go R and follow the lane to a TJ just before Newbridge rail crossing. Turn L at the TJ, go over the crossing and continue into Pickering about 1 mile along the road.

Once you are back in Pickering, you can either take the turning on the turning on the right shortly after the station, which is a minor road, or carry on to the A170, turning R at the roundabout to ride the remaining 2.5 miles back to the start in Aislaby.

Stream crossing in the woods below Newton-on Rawcliffe.

USEFUL CONTACTS

Mountain Bike Clubs

The West Yorkshire Rough Riders
This is possibly one of the best Mountain Bike Clubs in Yorkshire, catering for all abilities of rider. They draw their members from Leeds, Bradford, Halifax, Huddersfield, and the Sheffield area. Their off-road riding takes place throughout the whole of Yorkshire and includes weekday evening rides as well as long weekends away. New members are always welcome and are initially looked after by a mentor. Annual Continental tours are also arranged. The club meets regularly at its clubhouse to discuss future rides.

Contacts:	Tony Vangrove	01484 662551
	Derek Boocock	01274 652301

North Yorkshire Jorvik Mountain Bike Club
This is also a well-established club, catering for families as well as riders interested in competition. Again, you can expect a warm welcome from members.

Contact::	Jake Goddard	01904 670132

North-East Mountain Bike Assoc. (NEMBA)

Contact	The Secretary, 68 Heidelberg Rd, Heaton, Bradford, West Yorks BD9 5EB

Hull Thursday C.C. (Mountain Bike Section)

Contact	01377 217850 OR 01482 708880

C.T.C. (York Representative)

Contact	01904 791700 OR 01904 654114

Huddersfield Star Wheelers
This is a well-established cycling club which has recently embraced mountain biking. They offer Saturday rides for beginners of all ages and Sunday rides for more experienced riders. They also cater for racing enthusiasts and promote a series of local races.

      Contact::   Ian Hodgkinson   01484 683437

Other contacts
The Cycling Officer, City of York Council, Environmental & Development Services, 9 St Leonards Place, York YO1 2ET; tel 01904 613161

York Cycle Campaign, c/o York Cycle Works, 14-16 Lawrence St, York; tel 01904 626664

TOURIST INFORMATION CENTRES
Helmsley	01439 770173
Malton	01653 600048
Pickering	01751 473791

The main Tourist Information Centres in York are at the Railway Station and another a short distance from it at Rougier St. The York Cycle Route Maps can be obtained from these centres. The maps provide an excellent street guide for cyclists in York City and even show access points for the off-road links.